EDGE OF THE LAGOON

By the same author:

Perspectives in Education, 1970.

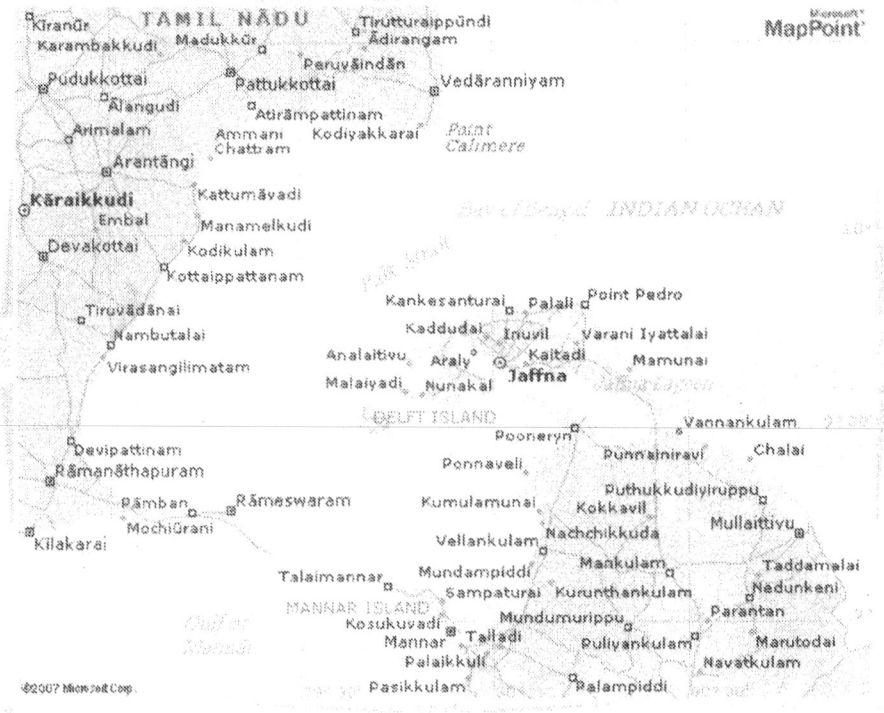

A map of Palk Strait, Tamil Nadu in South India, and the Jaffna Peninsula.

EDGE OF THE LAGOON

◆

SOME PERSPECTIVES OF JAFFNA

K. PARAMOTHAYAN

iUniverse, Inc.

New York Lincoln Shanghai

EDGE OF THE LAGOON
SOME PERSPECTIVES OF JAFFNA

iUniverse books may be ordered through booksellers or by contacting:

iUniverse
2021 Pine Lake Road, Suite 100
Lincoln, NE 68512
www.iuniverse.com
1-800-Authors (1-800-288-4677)

Because of the dynamic nature of the Internet, any Web addresses or links contained in this book may have changed since publication and may no longer be valid.

The views expressed in this work are solely those of the author and do not necessarily reflect the views of the publisher, and the publisher hereby disclaims any responsibility for them.

ISBN: 978-0-595-46733-4 (pbk)
ISBN: 978-0-595-70463-7 (cloth)
ISBN: 978-0-595-91028-1 (ebk)

Printed in the United States of America

To my children, Shanthi, Ajanta, Brinda and Rabindra;
sons-in-law, Ahilan and Peter;
daughter-in-law, Izabela;
and grandchildren, Arujunan, Sanjeevan, Kaja, Antek, Euan and Priya.

Contents

List of Illustrations

Foreword

"Tea from Ceylon!"—those were the words that still ring in my ears from advertisements in the 'fifties, and they always evoked a picture of a magical, exotic island world with acres of rich green tea bushes somewhere beyond the swelling rollers of the Indian ocean. Today "Sri Lanka" doesn't sound as romantic—but if I were to visit that land, I would be sure to take with me a copy of Dr Paramothayan's book. The title *Edge of the Lagoon* are words, once again, to conjure with! And indeed, the book takes one to the heart of that magical, though turbulent land with its ancient myths and rich mixture of cultures. And it's in Jaffna, in the northern apex of that triangular land just 22 miles from the southern tip of India, that one finds the descendants of the Tamils who gave the English language such enticing words as *catamaran, cheroot, corundum, curry, mango* and *mulligatawny,* and who also, as the author points out, gave us words like *anaconda* for a constrictor-boa, *coolie* for labourer, and *pariah* and *pariah dog* (pyedog) for the outcast and the downtrodden! For we will find in this land not only the best of civil servants, accountants and lawyers and teachers, but also the downtrodden, the poor and the exploited, victims, indeed, of a demagogic democracy where the Tamils, the energetic settlers from South India over many centuries, have in effect been swamped by the overriding authoritarianism of a government comprised of the indigenous majority where the old caste system still casts its long shadows across the land—a government with its deliberate policy of virtually disinheriting the Tamils, and other minority groups, of their fundamental rights as citizens of the country.

This is a meticulous, academic, well-researched study or exploration of the region and the country, well supported by meticulous and accurate footnoting and quotations from the people who have shaped the country. Indeed, the author has himself been a participant in that shaping, in its educational development especially, but also has been a fighter for justice and true democracy where every culture has the freedom to express its religion and the right to use its language as an official language of the country, regardless of whether the members of that culture are in the majority or minority. As the author says, with a substantial proportion of common blood running through the veins and arteries of Tamils (who are in the minority), Sinhalese (the major population group), and the Veddhas on the point of extinction, one is led to wonder if the administration of the DNA Test, which is commonplace in the contemporary world to solve longstanding claims, mysteries and puzzles, would help to resolve the problem of ethnic chauvinism in Ceylon too!

Throughout the book the author makes valuable comparisons with other social and government models, by way of elucidating and clarifying the present condition of Jaffna as well as its potential for the future. Belgium, for instance, is presented as a good model for Ceylon to have emulated at the time of her independence. "After the Second World War, the main task for the country was recognised as one of strengthening the nation by building bridges across its ethnic divisions. The Pact of Egmont negotiated in 1977 recognised three semi-autonomous regions, that of the Flemings in the north, the Walloons in the south, and cosmopolitan Brussels, the capital. Later, however, under a constitution hammered out in 1993, the regions of Flanders, Wallonia, and Brussels were granted greater autonomy, and Flemish, French and German recognised as official languages." So why not the same possibilities for Sri Lanka, where no racial or cultural group is dominated by another? But the truth is, there are very few countries in the world today that can claim to be true democracies. I have even heard Britain being described as "a benevolent dictatorship", and indeed, with the horrendous burden placed on its unwary citizens by the capital gains tax, for instance, Britain can hardly be seen as a benevolent democracy—for it is a country where businessmen as well as the ordinary citizens are obliged to be bled by accountants to prevent themselves from falling into the pitfalls of a taxation system imposed by the Westminster government on all of its peoples, whether they be part of a majority of supporters in the home counties or the powerless 'minorities' in the Outer Hebrides. Dr Paramothayan, himself a victim of majority aggression in his home country, presents facts and arguments in a way that stimulates the mind to think of similar injustices elsewhere. It is especially in his epilogue that he touches on the raw nerves of injustice, where he so expertly draws together the various threads of this tour de force of historical Ceylon and the socio-cultural and political elements of present-day Sri Lanka with remarkable insight and clarity.

As the author says, it would be difficult, perhaps, for those who are not so familiar with the comprehensive history of Ceylon, especially the situation in which the Tamils find themselves, to understand how a people with a rich cultural heritage, who had made Ceylon their home over so many centuries, and contributed in such large measure to the development of the country through many centuries, prior to and after colonial rule, were left high and dry within a few years of independence, with offensive, and often racially abusive labels attached to them. But thanks to this book the reader will have a comprehensive survey, a veritable tour de force of the country, a book that puts into perspective its historical roots, its physical environment, its brilliant educational heritage, its cultural, literary and religious wealth, as well as the social and political environment—a perspective that will enable the reader to better understand the situation in which the Tamils find themselves today.

The author never flinches from the truth. In the first instance he reveals the rich educational history that shaped the peoples of Jaffna. Education, standing as it does on the bedrock of philosophical idealism, including religious scholasticism, came to be deeply ingrained in the psyche of the Jaffna Tamils through centuries of contact with South India and the wider world it opened up. The educational experience of the average Tamil child involved listening to a series of folk tales, songs and verses etc. inculcating religious, moral and social obligations, and participating in ceremonies, including those associated with initiation into learning and adulthood. They were also open to the benefits introduced by the Christian missionaries, and missionary initiatives were embraced with open arms. It is clear that, retrospectively, unlike so many people in Africa, the people of Jaffna did not look upon the colonial missionaries as agents that "hijacked" their religion, since, when it came to Hinduism with its tolerance of different paths to perfection, the people saw the value of opportunity, and absorbed much of the educational stimulus of the missionaries to enrich their lives and lifestyles. There is no doubt that in the competition for jobs in the government and the private sector as well as in the leading professions, the Jaffna Tamils did have an edge over the rest of the country by virtue of the educational provision in the district—so that when the University College and later the University of Ceylon were set up in Ceylon, the Jaffna Tamils were not slow to take the initial advantage, with the schools rising to the occasion to cater to the ever increasing demand for access to university education.

With equal frankness, the author casts his critical searchlight on the newly created so-called co-operative organisations, beginning with the multi-purpose co-operatives, which came to be directly controlled by the government. (And people wonder why "government" corrupts everything it touches, and why it doesn't fix the problems of society—an age-old complaint of political journalists and satirists!) As Dr Paramothayan points out, Jaffna had the distinction of having its Member of Parliament appointed as President of the Jaffna Multi-Purpose Co-operative Society! (Because he—the author—was critical of governmental meddling in areas such as education and the co-operative movement, largely through newspaper columns and public speeches, he was told by the Member of Parliament—President of Jaffna MPCS—in no uncertain terms, that the Minister had made enquiries about him!) If Jaffna, the author says, is to recover from its present state of dominance by a majority government, it calls for nothing short of a rethink of the political landscape of the country, devolution of power being an essential pre-requisite.

The author felt a need to become an exile from his beloved Jaffna, having made Britain his new home to escape the strident and very aggressive racial ethos that began to emerge after independence. With maturity, however, the author hopes that Jaffna will be able to bring about a revolution of ideas aimed at creating an egalitarian society through genuine community participation at all levels. Before Jaffna, as he points out, there lies a long and tortuous road of honest toil and genuine sacrifice, but the goal of re-building and reclaiming a proud and precious homeland is worth any price. And this book, with its searching and deep insight into the Tamil situation, will go a long way towards paving that road and making that worthy goal all the more achievable.

Charles H. Muller
MA (Wales), Ph.D. (Lond), D.Litt (OFS), D.Ed. (SA)

Diadem Books
www.diadembooks.com

Preface

In his scholarly work, *The Story of Civilization* (1935), Will Durant observed: "As family-rearing, and then writing, bound the generations together, handing down the lore of the dying to the young, so print and commerce and a thousand ways of communication may bind the civilizations together, and preserve for future cultures all that is of value for them in our own. Let us, before we die, gather up our heritage, and offer it to our children." I do not presume for a moment that my thoughts and ideas presented in this volume are by any means the ultimate truth, but at the same time, I have always had the urge to leave for our children, and through them, for future generations, a factual interpretation of our heritage. In so doing, it is my fervent hope that it will also alert the international community to some of the travesties and injustices perpetrated on the minority citizens of the country of my birth, more often than not, by discriminatory policies based on deliberate misrepresentation of facts.

When I was contemplating the task before me, I was fortunate to have come into contact with Dr. Charles H. Muller, who, from the very outset, did everything possible to encourage me to get on with my mission. His advice and guidance, and especially his candid observation, that my memories and experiences would constitute a valuable record of history, which, without being published, "would be lost for posterity!", helped me immensely. A great scholar and author in his own right, Dr. Muller's magnanimity in agreeing to write the Foreword for this book has undoubtedly bestowed on it the much needed recognition as a useful contribution to an understanding of ethnic issues in an international perspective. I am indeed grateful to him for his kind and valuable patronage, and would unhesitatingly recommend him to any prospective author, young or old.

It was the late Dr. J.H. Ollman of the International Co-operative Alliance Secretariat in London, who never tired of prevailing upon me, ever since I came to know him in 1972, to undertake a comparative study of Jaffna and its people, especially for the benefit of the international community. It grieves me a lot that he is not here to appreciate my belated efforts; nonetheless, I remember him with much love and gratitude for his unstinting help at all times, especially when I was working at the I. C. A. for a brief period, and subsequently, when I had to prepare and submit my M.Sc. Dissertation in rather adverse circumstances.

I cannot, of course, forget the invaluable help and guidance I received from the late Professor Brian Holmes, Emeritus Professor of Comparative Education at the University of London, while I was engaged in my Ph.D. research under his supervision. As I readily acknowledged in my thesis: "Although I have known him for many years as an outstanding Comparative Educationist in the tradition of Professor Nicholas Hans and Professor Joseph Lauwerys, it was in the last few years that I came to know him intimately—he is indeed a rare teacher of high calibre who provokes thinking, and I must acknowledge how much I benefited from his approach." I might add that my research under Professor Holmes' valuable guidance yielded the bulk of the material, as well as the inspiration for this book. My thanks are also due to the University of London, and the Institute of Education in particular, for facilitating the research.

Apart from my mother, Anna, who not only breathed life into me, but also gave me a lifelong love for literature and poetry, as well as an unshaken faith in the resurrected Christ, there were many father figures who constantly influenced my thinking, and in many ways, helped to forge my character and personality. To mention all of them is indeed unrealistic, but I cannot fail to mention a few; namely, the Rev. J.T. Arulanantham, Principal of St. John's College, a great educationist and visionary, who guided me in many ways; *Kalai Arasu* K. Chornalingam, the doyen of Tamil Drama in Ceylon, who shared with me some of the finer points of the histrionic art and later insisted that I should write the Foreword for his book on Tamil Drama in Ceylon, in a fatherly gesture of affection, in spite of my relative inexperience; S.J. Gunasegaram, scholar, poet, and philosopher, who guided and inspired me a great deal; Lyman Kulathungam, Vice Principal of Jaffna College, and Editor of the *Morning Star,* to which I contributed for many years; K. Nesiah, a Comparative Educationist of national and international repute, who drew me into the valuable discipline, and later introduced me to the Co-operative Movement; S. Handy-Perinbanayagam, from whose fountain of knowledge and experience I could drink freely; T.Seenivasagam, journalist and long serving President of the Textile Union, who gave me an insight into the lives of the 'Common People'; Canon S. S. Somasundaram, the great Anglican priest, who generously took over the guardianship of my mother after she had lost her father as an infant, and her mother at eight, and showed the community by sheer example of simplicity and dedication what it meant to be a true disciple of Christ; Tori De Souza, Editor of *The Times of Ceylon,* who readily published a series of my contributions for more than a decade, and provided me with a valuable platform to draw public attention to issues relevant to the welfare of the nation; A.E. Tamber, the well known teacher, Trade Unionist, and champion of the underdog, whose backing at all times gave me the resilience to take on some of the tyrants and bullies, and also challenge unscrupulous politicians, who sought to level down some of the best institutions in Jaffna, including schools, hospitals and co-operatives, claiming to bring about 'equality of opportunity'; and, Dr. S.A. Vettivelu, the good physician and patriot, who constantly urged me to seek new opportunities abroad for my own welfare and safety.

I owe so much to my children, children-in-law, and grandchildren, for their immeasurable help and encouragement at all times, in the face of far too many unforeseen obstacles that cropped up from time to time, to ensure that I did not falter in the task that I had set before me. As a mark of love and gratitude I dedicate this book to them. It is also intended to signify that the book is, in the main, addressed to the younger, and by implication, future generations of Tamils, wherever they happen to find themselves!

My grateful thanks are also due to my Lord and Saviour, Jesus Christ, for the Love He bestowed on me throughout my rather difficult and demanding life, and for His succour and sustenance to the very end.

K.P.
September 2007

Introduction

FIREWOOD GATHERERS

Bevies of women petite
Elegant in their gait
Emerging from the woodlands
With bundles of firewood;
Sorted and neatly secured,
Carried on weary heads.

Smarting in the swelt'ring heat
Swathed in remnants modest,
Swaying gracefully homeward
Is a sight to behold!
A moving panorama
Of virtue in penury!

Professor K. Kanapathipillai's description above of an everyday scene in a typical village in the Jaffna Peninsula in Northern Sri Lanka, in one of his verses written in Tamil folk idiom, gives a vivid picture of village life in the Peninsula from time immemorial.

The virtue he describes is that of sheer industry in rather adverse circumstances. Edged on by the lagoon, perhaps, which separates the Peninsula from the mainland, the people of Jaffna had earned a reputation for industry under comparatively unfavourable conditions. Many an independent observer had commented on it, but the observations of Harry Williams are most striking:—

> "It is an astonishing place, the Holland of the East, and its people have acquired very much the same reputation for thrift, common sense and indefatigable energy that the Scots have won for themselves in every quarter of the world.... Closer inspection will reveal a hive of industry north of Elephant Pass, village upon village, all neat, clean and vigorous, with thousands of acres of tobacco plantations, highly cultivated market gardens producing

chillies, brinjals, ginger, melons, cassava, sweet potatoes, yams and other vegetables, with acres of beautiful flower gardens. After the indifferent husbandry and slothful lack of pride of the Sinhalese villagers, this intensive cultivation is an object lesson in what can be done, particularly as rainfall is light, and droughts long and frequent. With all these handicaps, industry and energy have produced a prolific countryside, comparable to the best to be found in Java, where a desert might reasonably have been expected ..."[1]

Apart from geographical separation coupled with a harsh climate, there were other major factors too, notably historical and socio-cultural as well as environmental and educational, that played a significant role in determining the psyche of the inhabitants of Jaffna, mainly Tamils.

Professor E.F.C. Ludowyk sums it up:—

"The Tamils ... were as a result of their geographical separation from the rest of the country, and the industry with which they profited from secondary schooling in English, both more conservative in their life and more forward looking in their ideas than the Sinhalese. Hinduism, South Indian Hinduism in particular, could apparently present to the new mores of English culture a much more solid front than the Buddhism of the Low countryman....

"What was typical of the Tamil, then, and is perhaps true even at the present time, was the moral earnestness which comes from a life of constant effort. Nothing happened by chance, the smallest actions had significant moral overtones. Dr. Arnold would have found understanding pupils in most Jaffna Tamils, for, like him, they read sublime significance into every event...."[2]

The ensuing study will examine in some detail the key factors, some of them inter-related and/or inter-dependent, in the making of Jaffna.

---

1.   Williams, H., *CEYLON, Pearl of the East,* Robert Hale, London, 1950, pp 332-33.
2.   Ludowyk, E.F.C., *The Story of Ceylon,* Faber and Faber, London, 1967, pp 223-24.

1

HISTORICAL

Jaffna, the name by which the Northern Peninsula (and District) of Sri Lanka is known, is a derivative from the original Tamil name *Yalpanam,* changed first by the Portuguese to *Jaffnapatao* and later by the Dutch to *Jaffnapatam.* Various stories have been handed down by way of written accounts as well as oral history connecting the name *Yalpanam* with a blind minstrel, a maestro in the art of playing the ancient Tamil musical instrument, the *Yal*—a unique synthesis of the Lute and the Lyre—to whom *Yalpanam* was given as a gift by the son or grandson of the first king of Jaffna, *Ugra Singhan.*

From the accounts given in the *Kailaya Malai, a* Tamil poem that recorded the early history of Jaffna, and the *Yalpana Vaipava Malai,* the first historical work extant on Jaffna, it appears that the first sovereign ruler of Jaffna was *Ugra Singhan* from Kalinga in south-eastern India, who had his capital at *Kadiramalai* in Chunnakam. According to the latter work *Ugra Singhan* succeeded in conquering many territories outside Jaffna by about 795 A.D. After completing the construction of the famous *Mavittapuram* temple, as a mark of gratitude to God for having cured his wife of a facial malformation when she bathed in the *Keerimalai* tank, he moved his capital to *Sangadaka Nagar,* identified by many authorities as Singai Nagar, probably near or in Vallipuram, off Pt. Pedro in the northern extremity of Jaffna.

In the early centuries before and after Christ, the Jaffna Peninsula was known as *Naganadu* or *Nagativu* (Land or Island of the Nagas). As a matter of fact, but for the narrow embankment of coral beds and sand at Elephant Pass thrown up by the sea over the centuries, Jaffna could justifiably have been called an Island rather than a Peninsula. Indeed, Ptolemy's well-chronicled map of the second century A.D. named it *Nagadibi,* no doubt a corrupted form of *Nagativu.*

In his study of ancient and abandoned civilisations in south-east Asia and the causes for their demise, Rhoads Murphey observed:—

> "Only in Ceylon is there a more or less continuous historical record, plus numerous stone inscriptions to assist in solving the puzzle....
>
> "Tamil settlers who had been arriving off and on since before the Christian era, occupied the Jaffna Peninsula and much of the area between it and Anuradhapura, known as *Wanni* (as indicated by the large number of old Tamil place names in the *Wanni*); they had been joined by Tamil members of invasion armies, often mercenaries, who chose to settle in Ceylon rather than return to India with the rest of the army ..."[1]

The fortunes of the Jaffna kingdom, therefore, inevitably changed with turbulent changes in South India. The Cholas in particular, who were a constant threat, brought the kingdom of Rajarata under their rule by the end of the tenth century, and by the beginning of the eleventh century succeeded in proclaiming the entire Island a province of the world-famous Chola empire. The *Yalpana Vaipava Malai* asserts that for about four centuries following the Chola occupation, the kingdom of Jaffna exercised sovereign power over the whole of North Ceylon, especially under the Pandya rulers, the *Aryachakravartis,* who gradually extended their influence along the western seaboard.

In fact, Ibn Batuta, the Arab itinerant who visited Ceylon in 1344, wrote that Arya Chakravarthi, the Tamil king of Jaffna, was the greatest king in the Island with a powerful fleet commanding the western coast, with whose help and protection he was able to undertake the pilgrimage to Adam's Peak through Chilaw, returning via Kale (Galle) and Kolanbu (Colombo), which he described as the best and biggest city in *Serendib.*

After a great deal of sustained resistance by Jaffna with the support of various groups and alliances, from within and without, the kingdom finally yielded to the Portuguese might in 1621, mainly as a consequence of internecine rivalry and intrigue.

From then on until the gaining of independence by Ceylon in 1948, in the wake of the liberation of India, Jaffna, like the rest of the country, with the exception of Kandy which succeeded in resisting Portuguese and Dutch rule until at last it

---

1.   Murphey, R., The Ruin of Ancient Ceylon, *Journal of Asian Studies*, April 1957, pp 181-82.

fell to the British in 1815, was ruled for almost three and a half centuries by three European powers in succession—the Portuguese, the Dutch and the British.

The Portuguese during their comparatively brief spell of rule were the most ruthless, in that they embarked on a deliberate mission of suppressing local religion and culture by destroying Hindu temples, traditional educational institutions and pockets of local resistance. Paradoxically though, they left behind a solid base of institutions like churches, schools, hospitals and law courts for the Dutch to build on. The Dutch provided the added infrastructure, in particular a codified legal system incorporating the *Thesavalamai,* the customary laws of Jaffna, a more liberal and progressive educational structure and a more modern communications system. The British rule turned out to be, on the whole, a blessing in disguise to an ailing country in many ways. The introduction of the fundamental principles of the Rule of Law and Freedom of Speech, and other liberal reforms in administration, economic management and education, most of them prompted by changes in Britain itself, should have had far reaching consequences, but for irresponsible leadership from the very first steps into independence.

In a valuable study, Ralph Pieris speaks of the "blind alley civilisations" of the East, which had to remain at the stage of archaism until some alien power stepped into the breach to perform for the ailing society the reforms that were long overdue.[2]

There was the example of India who got her well-earned independence a year before Ceylon, but the latter clearly failed from the very outset in its most important task of nation building. Whereas the fathers of the Indian Constitution adopted an "India in microcosm" approach in drafting the constitution, incorporating a whole series of fundamental rights for the protection of minority interests, Sri Lanka, in sharp contrast, continues to pay the price for a lackadaisical and partisan approach to constitution making and nation building.

There can be no doubt that when a country lacks the rudiments of intellectual honesty and sound leadership, it really does risk its future.

---

2. Pieris, R., Society and Ideology, 1795-1850, *University of Ceylon Review*, Vol. IX, pp 3-4.

2

ENVIRONMENTAL

Jaffna is the second largest of the three administrative Districts of the Northern Province of Sri Lanka, with a land area of around 1000 square miles, the others being Vavuniya with 1470 square miles and Mannar with 965 square miles.

The Jaffna District, comprising the Jaffna Peninsula and the adjoining islands, eleven in number, is separated from the mainland by the lagoon at Elephant Pass with a total spread of roughly 300 square kilometres.

Being a continuation of peninsular India, both geologically and geographically, the Jaffna District is made up almost entirely of crystalline rocks of the Archaen age, the geological period pertaining to the earlier part of the Precambrian era, estimated to be more than 600 million years old. These rocks are predominantly metamorphosed with an intrusion of gneiss, schist and granite. The entire Jaffna Peninsula and the associated islands are also floored by limestone of sedimentary origin dating back to the Miocene age, i.e., more than 30 million years ago, when it formed the bed of the sea that covered the north-west fringe of Ceylon and the southern peripheries of India. Later on, with the shrinking of the sea over subsequent periods, it was exposed as dry land. Palk Strait, the narrow inlet of the Bay of Bengal that separates Jaffna from Tamil Nadu in South India and Adam's Bridge, the short stretch of shoals providing the historical link between Sri Lanka and epic India, are probably the remains of that ancient sea of the Miocene age.

As a consequence of its geological origin, Jaffna is a domain of salt water with coasts broken up by inlets and small lagoons, no place in the peninsula being more than 40 or 50 miles from the sea. The soil in Jaffna is, therefore, on the whole saline, with the exception of the red soils of the interior. They are the remnants of limestone deposits dissolved by rainwater over long periods of time and owe their reddish-yellow colour to traces of iron, which make them fertile.

Situated within ten degrees of latitude to the north of the Equator, Jaffna is subject to the equatorial climatic phenomena. However, as a comparatively tiny peninsula exposed to the vagaries of weather conditions in the Bay of Bengal, it is subject to a rather inclement climatic environment.

Jaffna experiences high temperatures averaging about 81.5 degrees Fahrenheit and an annual rainfall ranging from 40 to 60 inches, most of it concentrated in the three months from October to December. It is subject, therefore, to long periods of drought accompanied by strong winds, infrequently gale force, and cyclones. In spite of the seasonal sea and land breezes, loss of humidity through evaporation is a serious problem to be reckoned with.

The inevitable shortage of fresh water would have had serious consequences for Jaffna, but for the bed of sedimentary limestone rocks. They are permeable, riddled with numerous cracks, crevices and joints and as such act as good aquifers or water bearers, helping to conserve a substantial reservoir of underground fresh water. Where temperatures are high and rainfall minimal, and where loss of moisture through evaporation is a serious threat to plant, animal and human existence, such permanent settlements as are found in Jaffna, would not have been possible but for the subterranean reservoir of fresh water that could be tapped by sinking wells. These wells provide water for irrigation as well as for drinking and other general purposes. There are a couple or more of natural springs too, the most famous of them at Keerimalai, historically renowned for its health giving qualities as well as miraculous powers.

There is, of course, the paramount need to keep the fresh water table underground at an optimum level. This is done mostly by natural water bodies, such as ponds and pools, into which excess rainwater collects and gradually percolates into the sub-surface limestone bed, thereby raising the level of the fresh water table. Most of these water bodies are natural features of the landscape formed by rainwater acting on limestone, gradually dissolving it and causing hollows and passages to be formed, which become enlarged over time. In rare instances, the entire sub-surface limestone roof can collapse, as in the case of the popular well in Puttur. Hollows and depressions are also formed in sandy areas by the action of very strong winds that scoop away vast quantities of sand and deposit it as sand dunes elsewhere. They too serve as water retainers and feeders to the subterranean reservoir.

Nevertheless, unless an optimum balance of fresh water is maintained by artificial means as well, such as clearing of water beds of silt and sludge or clay from time to time, sea water is bound to seep into the rocks underneath, affecting the fresh water balance and gradually turning the water saline or brackish. Care is also needed to ensure that the delicate balance between the top layer of fresh water and the layer of saline water below is not disturbed by over use, especially by pumping out the water excessively.

Traditionally the clearing of waterbeds in ponds and pools etc. was done by farmers and/or local artisans, the former to use the silt and sludge to fertilise their land and the latter to use the clay for pottery and other artistic purposes. In communally owned water facilities there were always groups of local volunteers to undertake the essential task of maintaining the waterbeds free of silt, sludge or clay.

In more recent times, however, due to demographic changes as well as changes to farming methods, not to mention consequential occupational and social mobility, clearing of waterbeds has inevitably gone into neglect, resulting in not only a gradual increase in the salinity of the sub-surface water reserve, but also an increased risk of flood damage. The long-term impact of this on the environment and its implications for the fauna and flora in general, and public health in particular, are no doubt a matter of great concern.

Some water bodies, especially in the town centre, have been neglected over so many years that they are extremely putrid and toxic, to say the least, and a veritable health hazard. An ardent student brought home the point in one of his responses to a survey questionnaire, when he expressed his strong reservation as follows: "… they are not well maintained by the authorities, and there are many diseases spreading due to *insanity!*"[1]

In any case, public health has always been a thorny problem in Jaffna, mainly as a consequence of central government control and local government inertia, ably assisted by public apathy. Hence sanitation was the least of the priorities in Jaffna, with virtually no provision for even basic amenities like public lavatories. What is even more disturbing is the long history of complacency, neglect and squandering of public money on ill thought out projects.

A class of low caste and downtrodden people brought down from India specifically to perform the loathsome task of removal and disposal of human excrement

---

1.   Paramothayan, K., *Perspectives in Education*, Lake House, Colombo, 1970, p.37.

from homes was in itself inhuman, sordid and unhygienic, but an altogether unjust and extravagant practice assumed ugly proportions under corrupt and inept local government administration. Well into the 1960s or even later, one could witness the filthy environment just behind the Jaffna Municipal Council premises, including the Town Hall. It was one of the most neglected areas in the town centre with push carts, buckets and other paraphernalia of the sewage disposal culture displayed prominently, against the background of a desecrated cemetery, grotesque structures of a handful of abandoned and vandalised public lavatories where they shouldn't have been built in the first place, by the beach, and dirty open drains struggling to empty into the sea.

What was particularly disconcerting to the general public was that a sewage disposal scheme for the Jaffna Municipal area, including the Jaffna Hospital, was already conceived and planned by health officials by the early 1950s, but failed to get the go-ahead from the Council, time and again, due to petty political bickering.

Illegal alcohol booths and breweries and ad hoc industries that pollute the environment abound in the city. Stray dogs, often rabid, and cattle on the spree, are a common sight; apparently they have formed a tripartite alliance with the ubiquitous crows to keep the city clear of garbage!

The picture, however, is not so dismal as it might sound. There are open spaces, parks and gardens, and also a few significant historical sites, although some of them have been damaged or partially destroyed in the civil conflict of recent years.

The most important of these sites is the Jaffna Fort on the edge of the Jaffna lagoon. Originally built by the Portuguese, it was rebuilt by the Dutch and renovated by the British. Mostly built of breccia, or reshaped coral stones, some of them showing markings of marine organisms, it is an imposing structure commanding a vast landscape, including the magnificent esplanade with its clock tower on one side and the lagoon on the other. There is some evidence of pillage and looting too with a few stones bearing the imprints of Hindu religious symbols, such as the lotus, indicating that they had been removed from temples after they had been razed to the ground by the Portuguese.

Within the extensive premises of the Fort, surrounded by massive walls, there are a few buildings, including the invaluable Dutch church, partly destroyed, containing priceless mementos like the original Portuguese church bell bearing the inscription *Nossa Senhora dos Milagres de Jaffnapatao* ('Our Lady of the Miracles of Jaffna'), the Organ Gallery, the chalice style pulpit and an amazing array of granite tombstones, the vast majority of them Dutch. Within the ramparts of the Fort are also the Governor's Residency and other administrative buildings of the colonial era.

Jaffna Fort

The Organ Gallery in the Dutch Church

The 'Chalice' model Pulpit

A Tombstone of 1672 in the Dutch Church
within the premises of the Jaffna Fort

The Dutch apparently had a special affinity to Jaffna, perhaps due to some striking similarity to their homeland eliciting a sense of nostalgia. The numerous Dutch names they bestowed so lavishly speak for themselves, as, for instance, the names given to most of the islands off the coast of Jaffna, like Amsterdam, Rotterdam, Haarlem, Middleburgh, Leyden, Delft and Kayts, some in vogue to this day.

The Dutch were also more restrained in their attitude towards Hindu temples than the Portuguese before them. Of significance is the most important Hindu temple in Jaffna, the Nallur Kandaswamy Temple, which was damaged during

Portuguese rule several times, and later used by the Portuguese as their headquarters until the Jaffna Fort was completed. Restored subsequently by the Dutch, it bears some features of Dutch renaissance architecture, and is undoubtedly the most important cultural landmark in Jaffna. The temple attracts thousands of devotees and other visitors of many faiths to its annual festivals, especially the colourful Chariot Festival during which Lord Kandaswamy is ceremoniously escorted in a colossal chariot (*Ther*), lavishly decorated, and drawn by hundreds of devotees. Indeed, it has been a unifying force throughout the centuries.

The popular Hindu Temple in Nallur, Jaffna.

The British who took over from the Dutch, however, became the unconscious tool of history that transformed the environment in every sense. Clutching to the Liberal Ideology and the Protestant Ethic as their only hope of a sheet anchor in the stormy seas generated by the Industrial and French Revolutions, Great Britain was indeed a *civilisation on the march*, which left its indelible mark on many a society around the world, especially those that sought to benefit from a confrontation with a progressive culture and a rich language. Jaffna did, and is the richer for it.

In spite of its turbulent history, people return to Jaffna in ever increasing numbers, mainly to 'breathe the Jaffna air', as they put it. The thirst-quenching young coconut, the fresh juice of the Palmyra palm, the many varieties of mangoes, plantains, papaw and other exotic fruits, and the wide choice of vegetables and fish are attractions in themselves. But the most important determinant of the environment in Jaffna is the ethos derived from a liberal intellectual tradition, enhanced by a relentless work ethic.

A sand dune in Jaffna. The Palmyra (*Borassus flabellifer*), a variant of Portuguese 'palmeira' (palm tree), is a time-honoured palm of Tamil history, literature, folklore, poetry, proverb and idiom, which has therefore earned a place in the Tamil psyche; also for its multifarious gifts of nature. Only the Palmyra can thrive on sand dunes.

3

SOCIO-CULTURAL

When Jaffna came under foreign rule almost four hundred years ago, there was already a well-established intellectual tradition nurtured by regular cultural contacts with the Indian sub-continent over many centuries.

T.P. Meenakshisunderam, quoting from Diole's *4000 Years Under The Sea,* dramatically described the maritime activities of the early Tamils, when he addressed the All India Oriental Conference held in Annamalainagar in 1955. Diole, he said, had depicted those Tamils as 'a half-way house people', who, in pre-historic times, had watched the ships coming from the West and had loaded them for the return journey with what their own ships had brought from China and Ceylon ...

"They had known at one and the same time the civilisation of the West and the civilisation of China—thanks to their familiarity with the sea."[1]

Milton Singer, the well-known anthropologist, puts it in a cultural context when he says:

"The chief sources of the early European image of India were the luxury trade through the Middle East and the accounts of travellers. The objects in the luxury trade—pepper, cinnamon, nutmeg, cloves, gold, diamonds, pearls, precious stones, ivory, silks and cottons—spoke for themselves. Many of the European words for these objects are loan words from the Indian languages. The English word 'India' itself carries the traces of the old trade routes, for it comes from the Latin 'India' which can be traced from the Greek 'Indike' through the Persian 'Hindu' back to the Sanskrit 'Sindhu', the name the ancient Indians gave to the Indus River. Pliny complained that

---

1.   Meenakshisunderam, T.P., (All India Oriental Conference, 1955), *Tamil Culture,* Vol. 5, No.2, Tamil Cultural Society, Colombo 1955, p 142.

the trade with India was draining Rome's treasury. In some cases, India was not the original source of the luxuries but only an entrepot, for some of the spices, precious stones, and gold came from Ceylon, Indonesia, and the Malay Peninsula."[2]

Besides, three *Sangams*, or Academic Associations for the promotion of Tamil language and literature, existed in South India from the third century BC onwards. Only the works of the third *Sangam*, extending over a period of about 2000 years, have survived, although *Tolkapiam*, the earliest work on Tamil grammar extant, is claimed by some scholars to have been written towards the beginning of the second *Sangam* period.

U.D. Jayasekara has observed:—

"A Tamil poet from Ceylon is said to have adorned the Tamil *Sangams* at Madhura—Ilattu Putan Tevanar. Seven of his poems are included in the *Sangam* Anthologies, *Akananuru, Kuruntokai* and *Nattinai*."[3]

The early part of the fifteenth century has been described by some commentators as the 'Augustan Age' of literary development in Jaffna, when a *Sangam* was established by the king at Nallur, the capital of the Tamil kingdom. Under the auspices of the *Sangam* many literary works were published. The *Sangam* also collected and preserved ancient Tamil classical writings and encouraged translations and adaptations from Sanskrit literature. Promising writers and scholars were also encouraged to go to South India to work with eminent *Gurus* in order to enhance their scholarship.

The fillip given to learning had the effect of spreading literacy, informally though, among the population at large, mainly through the oral tradition. It also helped to promote and preserve a pure form of Tamil considered peculiar to Jaffna. According to Father Xavier S. Thani Nayagam, "Tamil speech as obtaining in Ceylon, and Tamil phonetics as obtaining especially in the Northern and Eastern Provinces show a fidelity to the earliest Tamil grammars which the speech of South India does not—a clear indication of the development of Tamil

---

2. Singer, M., *WHEN A GREAT TRADITION MODERNIZES: An Anthropological Approach To Indian Civilization*, Praeger Publishers, N.Y., 1972, p14.

3. Jayasekara, U.D., *Early History of Education in Ceylon*, Department of Cultural Affairs, Ceylon, 1969, p 164.

in Ceylon unhampered by the extraneous influences to which South India was subject."[4]

The intellectual pursuit inevitably had its impact on folk idiom too, as seen in the rich folklore distinctive to Jaffna, and distinguishable in many respects from that of the sub-continent. Of the many forms of folklore like tales and legends, proverbs and parables, and those transmitted through myth and custom, the folk songs are the most enduring for their pathos and simplicity. Most are sung by those in extreme emotional situations, as, for instance, the lament of the widows:—

(a)   Wouldn't I have come running, if I'd known
                The pathway to your new household;
                Wouldn't I have rushed over, if I'd known
                The gateway to your new abode?

(b)   The silks and muslins I adored
                Are replaced by cottons white,
                And my resplendent jewellery
                All stored in oblivion!

                All those multi-coloured sarees
                I prized and indulged in?
                The time has come alas to wear
                The Mannar calico![5]

The misery of young girls struggling to cope with their daily chores is well portrayed by these simple lines:—

(a)   Not dried and polished, the rice
                Is not ready for the pot,
                And it is a bitter toil
                To churn the buttermilk!

---

4.   Thani Nayagam, Xavier S., *Tamil Culture*, Vol. 4, No.4, Tamil Cultural Society, Colombo, 1955, p 347.
5.   A cheap variety of unbleached cotton cloth introduced by weavers from Calicut in South India and made in Mannar, a district in the Northern Province.

(b)   Motherless, I laboured all alone
              Polishing the grain in toil and tears,
              You marauding crow, you pilferer,
              Grab and go, if it agrees with you!

Valour is extolled too in many a folk song, as, for instance, where the young mother pines for her valiant husband:—

(a)   Combing the copious copse-wood
              Where the five-headed cobra broods
              For flowers bold and beautiful—
              Your father, Fearless Arjuna![6]

(b)   Bellowing seas, control your rage
              Inflaming my restlessness;
              Waters springing from stones of age
              Contain your overflowing;
              You shimmering moon, so cruel,
              Phase out your tormenting rays
              Till my *Neelakandan*[7] returns!

Children are considered as gifts from God and greatly cherished. As such, many songs are devoted to them. For instance,

(a)   I was lost and distraught
              Without the patter of small feet,
              When Lord Siva, discreet,
              Gave you, my son, Treasure so great!

(b)   With branches of the olive tree
              Still dripping with its soothing balm,
              A cradle will I make for you;
              With legs wrought out of pure gold,
              The cradle will I fit for you;
              With strings strung up of priceless pearls,
              The cradle will I drape for you!

---

6.   One of the two heroes in the *Bhagavad-Gita*.
7.   An appellation for Krishna, an incarnation of Vishnu, who preached to Arjuna on the battlefield in the *Bhagavad-Gita*.

(c)   Why weepest thou, who caused those tears
             Surging from thy crimson eyes?
             Make known the villain of the peace,
             In shackles strong he'll remain!

In traditional villages, most of the domestic chores like collecting firewood and polishing the grain were done by women, while men worked on the fields. Sometimes, tasks such as these would be undertaken collectively in return for wages.

Polishing the grain on a communal basis was common in some villages, where a mound would serve as a platform on which a large wooden mortar would be in place. Groups of women would go round the platform, singing rhythmically as they moved, polishing the grain in the mortar with long wooden pestles. Most of the songs would be of a lyrical kind, concerning subjects of common interest like love, dress, etc, but some could indulge in some gossip or innuendo too to break the monotony. The following is a typical example:—

             Polishing the stubborn grain
             Around the rounded mound,
             We spot a *Chayachoman*[8]
             Displayed in brilliant hue!

             How come by such luxury,
             Wonder, who's the lover?

             With hands sore in drudgery
             I earned my keep; without
             Bartering my chastity
             Wore my *Chayachoman*!

Tamil drama was largely influenced by developments in South India, but there were some forms of folk play that were indigenous. According to *Kalai Arasu* K.Chornalingam, there were two main forms of folk play, the *Nadagam* and the *Vilasam*. Whereas *Nadagam* was indigenous to Jaffna, the *Vilasam* type of folk play was in the main South Indian in origin and more popular in the Eastern Province, especially in Batticaloa, where it was called *Vadamody* (Northern Variety) to denote its Indian parentage.

---

8.   A highly prized dyed cloth made locally.

The songs, dances, costumes, and more especially the techniques of production, were different too. The *Nadagam* was performed on a square shaped stage, the *Annavy* (Director), the singers and the instrumentalists occupying one side, allowing the other three sides of the square to be accessible to the audience. The actors performed individually, with costumes designed specifically for that purpose.

The stage for the *Vilasam* was circular in shape, often raised by about two feet. The *Annavy* and the rest of the crew stood in the centre of the stage, allowing the actors to move around them, while the audience sat all round the stage.[9]

The Hindus of Jaffna are almost exclusively Saivites, i.e., worshippers of Siva, the supreme deity. His two sons Ganesha and Murukan, and his wife Parvati are worshipped too in their various manifestations. The most popular in Jaffna are the Murukan temples at Nallur, Maviddapuram and Selvasannathy, which attract thousands of devotees, especially during their annual festivals.

Annual Chariot Festival at the Nallur Temple.

---

9.   Chornalingam, K., *The Co-operator*, Jaffna, 15 June, 1968.

There are a handful of Vishnu temples as well, the most popular of them being the Vannai Perumal temple at Vannarpannai, Jaffna. Its history, like that of the temples at Nallur and Maviddapuram, provides valuable insight into the socio-cultural milieu of Jaffna.

E.F.C. Ludowyk writes:—

> "In the Jaffna district which was quieter and better controlled than almost any other part of their territories, the Dutch very soon tried to introduce weaving and the dyeing and painting of cloth. For this purpose weavers and printers were settled in Jaffna from the Coromandel coast. The root which produced the red dye—*Chaya* or Indian madder—was produced in Jaffna, and until the beginning of this century the distinctive Jaffna printed cloths were an article of trade. The Reverend Philip Baldaeus was apprehensive of the bad influence of these heathenish calico printers from India on his flock: 'It is further to be feared, that in time there may be a promiscuous copulation betwixt the Christians and Pagans, which must needs produce direful effects in the church.'"[10]

Events, however, proved that the fears of the Rev. P. Baldaeus were unfounded, for the weavers and printers from India not only brought their specialist handicraft with them, but their Vaishnava worship and practices as well, which enriched the indigenous culture. According to the history of the temple, Baldaeus had in fact repeatedly prevailed upon the Dutch authorities to ban all Hindu practices in Jaffna, including Vaishnava worship, but since the Dutch government had incurred considerable expenses in bringing down the weavers from India, they were rather reluctant to enforce the ban on Vaishnava worship for fear of antagonising the newcomers, which would have meant further losses for the Dutch Government.

The weaving community was able to draw sufficient inspiration from the *Perumal*[11] temple, which helped them to fortify themselves against all forms of pressures or persecution. In fact, the temple *Ther* (Chariot) had been designed in such a way as to function as an Art Gallery depicting religious and cultural themes that ordinary people could understand.[12]

---

10. Ludowyk, E.F.C., *The Story of Ceylon*, op. cit., p 127.
11. Another appellation for Vishnu.
12. Seenivasagam, T., *Sri Vengadesa Varatharajah Perumal Devasthanam*, Perumal Temple Mahasabai, Jaffna, 1960, pp 1-3, 18-20.

As Hinduism is not a centrally organised religion like Christianity or Islam, it did not have to resort to proselytism, which according to many authorities, accounts for its almost unique sense of tolerance. S. Radhakrishnan explains:—

"In religion, Hinduism takes its stand on a life of spirit, and affirms that the theological expressions of religious experiences are bound to be varied. One metaphor succeeds another in the history of theology until God is felt as the central reality in the life of man and the world.

"Hinduism repudiates the belief resulting from a dualistic attitude that the plants in my garden are of God, while those in my neighbours' are weeds planted by the Devil which we should destroy at any cost. On the principle that the best is not the enemy of the good, Hinduism accepts all forms of belief and lifts them to a higher level. The cure for error is not the stake or the cudgel, not force or persecution, but the quiet diffusion of light."[13]

Some guardian deities from the Hindu pantheon have been assimilated into the Sinhalese religious practices over the centuries, to the extent that they are worshipped by Buddhists and Hindus alike, and temples dedicated to those deities are popular with followers of both religions. The Murukan temple at Kataragama is a good example.

There is a vast body of Sinhalese literature dealing with *Pattini* worship in Ceylon, and most of it can be traced to Tamil sources, mainly the twin epics *Silappadikaram* and *Manimekalai*. *Kannagi*, the heroine of *Silappadikaram*, was deified as goddess *Pattini* during the reign of Senguttuvan, the *Cera* king of South India in the second century A.D. How *Pattini* worship came to be embraced by the Sinhalese is explained by Jayasekara:—

"Gajabahu is the hero of a considerable cycle of Sinhalese ballads and folk tales connected with the cult of goddess *Pattini*, still an important element in the religion of the Sinhalese ...
"The Tamil epic poem, *Silappadikaram*, which, according to some authorities, was composed in the second century and according to others, in the sixth or seventh century, and of which the subject matter is the story of *Kannagi*, deified as *Pattini*, refers to Gajabahu of Ceylon (Edited by Swaminatha Aiyar, Madras, 1920, pp 30 & 589). He is said to have been present

---

13. Radhakrishnan, S., *The Hindu View of Life*, Allen and Unwin, London, 1927, p 127 et seq.

on the occasion when Senguttuvan, the *Cera* king, consecrated a shrine in honour of *Pattini*, and established a place of worship to that goddess in his dominions. In the Sinhalese ballads, as well as the later historical work, the *Rajavaliya*, Gajabahu is said to have brought to Ceylon, on his return from the *Cola* country, the anklet of the goddess *Pattini* ...

"... it is said that on his return from South India he brought a large collection of books written in Tamil dealing with the cult and worship of *Pattini* (Gajaba-katava, v 59) ... and that the king caused these works to be read to him (see *Journal of the Royal Asiatic Society*, Ceylon Branch, Vol. xxviii, No.73, 1920, p 19)....

"The king may have perhaps gone a step further by either getting these works rendered in Sinhalese, or getting Sinhalese works composed in the light of the material available in the original Tamil works."[14]

The more plausible explanation for the dissemination of the *Pattini* cult among the Sinhalese is the cultural impact mainly through contact with Tamils and their literary traditions. According to Tamil tradition and oral history, Kannagi's husband, Kovalan, enticed by a dancing girl named Madhavi, dissipated the family fortunes. While trying to sell Kannagi's golden ankle-bracelet at Madurai, the capital of the Pandya kingdom, he was accused of stealing the queen's bracelet and unjustly put to death. Kannagi, distraught, tore away one of her breasts in anger, and by the power of her virtue invoked curses on the Pandya kingdom, and reduced the city of Madurai to ashes. Drought, famine and all kinds of pestilence followed, until one of the successor-kings appeased Kannagi by dedicating a temple to her memory, and celebrating a festival in honour of Kannagi, deified as *Pattini* (The Chaste). All other kings followed suit.

Gajabahu, king of Ceylon, who ascended the throne in 171 A.D., was a patron of Tamil literature. He is said to have been present at the consecration ceremony held at the *Cera* court of king Senguttuvan. On his return to Ceylon with a number of Tamil works, he is said to have had a temple consecrated to *Pattini*, where he made daily offerings, and decreed that a festival in honour of the new goddess be celebrated in the first month of each year. It is worthy of note, that the twin Tamil epics, *Silappadikaram* and *Manimekalai*, based on the stories of Kannagi and Madhavi respectively, have given rise to numerous legends and ballads, and a rich literary heritage in Sinhalese.

---

14. Jayasekara, U.D., *Early History of Education in Ceylon*, op. cit., pp 189-90.

Sinhalese and Tamil scholars have always agreed on the influence of Tamil on the Sinhalese language and culture. For instance, Father S. Gnana Pragasar, the eminent Tamil philologist, has pointed out that the old Tamil dialect as spoken in Jaffna "can still be seen in most of our place names especially in the north of the Island and in not a few ancient words of the Sinhalese language based, like other Indo-Aryan speeches, on a Dravidian substratum."[15]

Writing in the *Ceylon Historical Journal*, B.J. Perera observed:—

> "Tamil place names are found mostly along the sea-coast and in the Anuradhapura, Chilaw and Puttalam districts. Though there are no native Tamils living along the sea-coast south of Colombo, the Tamil origin of most of the present inhabitants there is seen from the fairly large number of Tamil place names. The 'ge' names of these people too attest to their Tamil origin. The word 'malai' meaning in Tamil 'a mountain or hill' is found in even the central parts of the island. They are come across in literature many centuries before the opening up of plantations and show that the Tamil element in the composition of the Sinhalese is far greater than is usually conceded. Ranmalaya, Kotmale, and Gilimale are some of the examples."[16]

'Kulam' is a Tamil word for a reservoir or tank, and many tanks in the Anuradhapura district have names ending with 'kulam' or 'kulama'. Other words in Tamil for a tank or pond are 'madu', 'kerni', 'odai', 'vil', etc. In the Vavuniya district, some villages owe their names to the tank or pond in the area, e.g., Ma*madu*, Nedun*kerni*, Maruth*odai*, and Kokka*vil*. It is also common for a tank or a pond to be named after the common flora in the area. *Puliyan*kulam, *Marutha*madu, *Nochi*kulam, Iranai-*iluppai*kulam, *Vilathi*kulam, and *Karunka-li*kulam are good examples.

The caste system, an integral part of Sanskritic Hinduism as practised in Jaffna, also had its impact on other religious groups like Buddhists and Christians. As Sydney Bailey explains:—

> "A caste was a Hindu social group, membership of which was decided by birth. An orthodox Hindu could not change from one caste to another,

---

15. Gnana Pragasar, S., Antiquity, Culture and Civilisation of the Ceylon Tamils, *The Co-operator*, Jaffna, 15 April, 1968.
16. Perera, B.J., Some Observations on the Study of Sinhalese Place Names, *The Ceylon Historical Journal*, Vol. 11, 1953, pp 241-50.

could not marry a person from another caste, could not eat or mingle socially with a person from another caste. At first there were only four castes—priests, warriors, merchants and craftsmen, and labourers. Gradually new caste distinctions were recognised. This Hindu system was introduced to Ceylon by the Tamils and was adopted by the Buddhist population. In the process, however, it became a less rigid institution than it had been on the Indian mainland, and during the nineteenth and twentieth centuries it began to break down under the impact of western ideas."[17]

The caste system in Jaffna was also associated with a form of slave labour used in agriculture. In the Sinhalese areas, as K.M. de Silva has pointed out, slave labour was domestic, whereas in Jaffna it was praedial, and on the whole, more oppressive. He also observed that the British Government, by a Proclamation dated 3 January 1821, abolished the Tamil slave-owners' right to kill or maltreat their slaves, but "despite their ultimate emancipation, there was no perceptible improvement in their position; they remained as despised and poverty-stricken as they originally were."[18]

No doubt, the caste system has been a baneful influence in Jaffna, eating away at the very fabric of society.

The confrontation with the English language, and the ideas it presented, had the effect of adding a potent catalyst to the socio-cultural milieu of Jaffna already in ferment. Many outstanding scholars and writers emerged mainly as a result of the new ethos engendered by English education. One such scholar was Arumuga *Navalar* (1822-1879), the first to be honoured with the title of *Navalar* (the Erudite) by the Thiruvavadu *Math*, the highly respected seat of Tamil scholarship in South India. He received his English education at Jaffna Central College, established by the Methodist Mission in 1834, where he later worked as a teacher. He wrote the first authoritative work on Tamil language and grammar, in addition to many other original treatises and commentaries. A Hindu reformer, he had no qualms in choosing to be a teacher in a Christian school, and even helping the missionaries in translating some of their tracts and pamphlets, as well as parts of the English bible into Tamil.

---

17.   Bailey, S.D., *CEYLON*, Hutchinson's University Library, London, 1952, p 36.
18.   De Silva, K.M., *Social Policy and Missionary Organizations in Ceylon* 1840-1855, Published for The Royal Commonwealth Society by Longmans,1965, p 209.

Sabapathy *Navalar* (1845-1903) was the second scholar to be honoured by the Thiruvavadu *Math,* and the first Jaffna Tamil to hold the post of Adeena *Vidwan* (Archetypal Scholar) at the *Math.* An erudite scholar in Tamil and Sanskrit, he lived in South India for many years producing a number of original works. He was also proficient in English.

Another luminary was Kumaraswamy *Pulavar* (Poet, 1855-1922). In addition to writing poetry of outstanding quality, he authored a number of learned commentaries. He received his education at Mallakam English school, and later acquired sufficient proficiency in English to be able to participate in the early efforts in Jaffna to compile a Tamil-English Dictionary. As a Member of the *Madurai Tamil Sangam,* he also made regular contributions to *Senthamil,* the monthly journal of the *Sangam.*

Somasunthara *Pulavar* (1876-1953) was a highly rated poet, an ardent Hindu social reformer and a teacher. With his substantial knowledge of English, he could have gone into more remunerative professions, but chose to be a teacher throughout his working life.

Jaffna was also the home of Dictionaries. The American Ceylon Mission that founded Jaffna College in 1827, and established the first Printing Press at Manipay in Jaffna, published the first Tamil-English Dictionary in 1842, called the *Manual Dictionary of the Tamil Language,* also popularly known as the 'Manipay Dictionary'. Dr. Miron Winslow's famous *Comprehensive Tamil and English Dictionary,* published in Madras in 1862, was also begun in Jaffna by Joseph Knight, with the assistance of the Rev. Peter Percival, the founder of Jaffna Central College, and other native scholars like Gabriel Tissera, and American Christian Missionaries like Levi Spaulding and Samuel Hutchings.

The first Encyclopaedia in Tamil was published by A. Mootootambipillai (1858-1917). Printed at the Navalar Press established by Arumuga *Navalar,* and entitled *Abidhana Kosam,* it was an invaluable contribution to Tamil scholarship, although, as the title suggests, it was heavily Sanskritised, in keeping with the trend of the time. He followed it up with the English-English-Tamil-Dictionary in 1907, dedicated to Dr. Ananda Coomaraswamy. One of his other major contributions was to translate the *Kailasa Malai,* one of the two historical works extant on Jaffna, and have it published in English in the *Ceylon National Review* in 1908. Already, the other historical work on Jaffna, the *Yalpana Vaipava Malai,* had been translated into English and published by C. Brito in 1879.

C.W. Kathiravelpillai was also a pioneer lexicographer, whose spadework with the help of Kumaraswamy *Pulavar*, blossomed as the *Sangath Thamil Agarathy* (Sangam Tamil Dictionary).

Father S. Gnana Pragasar, a pioneer comparative philologist, wrote a number of expert treatises and commentaries on Tamil language and culture, both in Tamil and English, which came to be widely acknowledged as authoritative works. He is best remembered for his *Studies in Etymology*, and *Etymological and Comparative Lexicon of the Tamil Language*.

Dr. Ananda K. Coomaraswamy, the renowned art critic, historian and authority on Indo-Ceylon Art and Aesthetics, came from a highly educated family in Jaffna. Having an English mother, too, might have helped him in his mastery of several languages and cultural nuances. He achieved international reputation for his books and commentaries, and is perhaps best remembered for his book, *The Dance of Shiva*, an aesthetic interpretation of cosmic balance, and a synthesis of Science, Religion, Philosophy and Art. His greatest contribution, however, was, like Rabindranath Tagore, to alert the world to a universal and integrated cultural heritage.

Ananda Tandava—Dance of Ecstasy
One of the most popular forms is the depiction of the Dance of Siva,
either in stone or bronze, as encircled by fire and trampling on the *Dwarf of Ignorance.*

The *Morning Star* was the first journalistic venture in Jaffna. Founded by the American Ceylon Mission in 1841 and printed at the American Mission Press, it was published as a bi-monthly in Tamil and English, and grew to maturity over the years, catering to a wide readership both within Jaffna and beyond. The Navalar Press, established by Arumuga *Navalar* in 1849, published a number of valuable books and commentaries in Tamil and English to cater to the increasing appetite of an educated and sophisticated audience, in addition to producing a substantial body of literature on Hinduism.

By about the seventh century there was a religious revival in India leading to the re-emergence of the *Bhakti* movement, which had had a long history of development. It was essentially devotional worship marked by song-offerings to the supreme deity, the Triad. A great number of religious poets wrote devotional songs of exceptional piety, passion and beauty between the seventh and eleventh centuries. Most of the songs at the beginning were devoted to Siva, but gradually songs in praise of the rest of the Triad, especially Vishnu, appeared, and attracted a very wide audience within and without India. Some of the most appealing songs came to be translated into English, thanks to the untiring work of Hindu as well as Christian scholars and missionaries.

The poet-saints who captured the imagination of the Jaffna populace were mostly those who wrote in praise of Siva, because of the predominance of Saivites, but in course of time, others too were well received and came to be appreciated.

Of the Saivite poets, Thirunavukkarasu, known as *Appar* and Gnanasambandar, known as *Sambandar*, who lived in the seventh century, and Manickavasagar (Vasagar) and Sundaramurthy (Sundarar), who lived in the eighth and ninth centuries respectively, became almost household names, and it became a common practice to sing their songs in religious ceremonies, even in some Christian circles. Many scholars, lay as well as clergy, were attracted to these lofty hymns, and popularised them by translating them into English. The following are excerpts from some translations:—

From *Vasagar*—

> There stand the players on the sweet-voiced lute and lyre;
> > There those that utter praises with the Vedic chaunt;
> There those whose hands bear wreaths of flowers entwined;
> > There those that bend, that weep, in ecstasy that faint;
> There those that clasp above their heads adoring hands;—
> > Shiva-Lord, in *Perun-turrai's* hallowed shrine Who Dwell'st!
>
> Me too make Thou thine own, on me sweet grace bestow!
> Our mighty Lord! FROM OFF THY COUCH IN GRACE ARISE!
>
> (*Tiruvacagam*, translated by Pope, G.U., Clarendon Press,
> Oxford, 1900, pp 207 et seq.)

Through re-interpretations and translations, well-known western scholars like G.U. Pope, R. Caldwell, B.V. Beschi and G.H. Westcott gave an incentive to Tamil cultural development in India, which had its immediate resonance in Jaffna.

From *Appar*—

1. Eyes of mine, gaze on Him
   Who drank the dark sea's bane.[19]
   Eight arms He brandishes in dance,
   At Him agaze remain.

   I sought Him and I found.
   Brahma sought in vain on high.
   Vishnu delved vainly underground.
   Him in my soul found I.

2. We are not subject to any; we are not afraid of death;
   We will not suffer in hell; we live in no illusion;
   We feel elated; we know no ills; we bend to none;
   It is all one happiness for us; there is no sorrow,
   For we have become servants, once for all,
   Of the independent Lord,
   And have become one at the beautiful flower-strewn
   feet
   Of that Lord.

From *Sundarar*—

I roamed, a cur, for many days
Without a single thought of Thee,
Roamed and grew weary, then such grace
As none could win Thou gavest me.
Venney-nallur, in "Grace's shrine"
Where bamboos fringe the *Pennai*, there
My shepherd, I became all thine;
How could I now myself forswear?

(*Hymns of the Tamil Saivite Saints*, Kingsbury, F.
and Phillips, G.E., YMCA Publishing House,
Association Press, Calcutta, 1921, pp 53 et seq.)

---

19. Refers to the churning of the ocean by Siva, when among the items churned up was
    a large quantity of deadly poison, which he drank in order to save humanity.

The Rev. Francis Kingsbury was a Tamil priest attached to the Church Missionary Society in Jaffna. He wrote many commentaries and translated many Tamil works, Christian and Hindu, into English, some in collaboration with others in Ceylon and India.

Many songs were written as offerings to Vishnu too, which provide the basis of devotional worship in many parts of India and Ceylon. Some later poet-saints showed a marked departure from traditional Hindu beliefs and practices, indicating the gradual impact of western education and ideas. Tukaram (1598-1649), for example, who wrote in Marathi, revolutionised traditional thinking, and was perhaps the first to break new ground by speaking out against the caste system and the theory of *karma*. Being of low caste himself, he believed in righteous living as the only way to break through the cycle of *karma* and rebirth, and attain union with a merciful God, capable of redemption. His poetry attracted a wide audience among all religious groups, and an English translation of his songs, published by the Christian Literature Society in Madras in 1909, attracted wide attention, especially among the depressed and the oppressed. T. Seenivasagam, a leading educationist and journalist in Jaffna, and a long-time leader of the weaving community, explained to the present writer how the songs of poet-saints like Tukaram, found an immediate resonance within his own community, who had to struggle for their survival in a conservative and caste-ridden society. Translations of their devotional songs became popular with worshippers at Vishnu temples. In one of his moving songs, Tukaram pleads:—

> I have been harassed by the world;
> I have dwelt in my mother's womb and I must enter the
>   gate of the womb eight million times.
> I was born a needy beggar and my life is passed under a
>   stranger's power.
> I am bound fast in the meshes of my past and its fated
> Influence continues with me;
> It puts forth its power and whirls me along.
> My stomach is empty and I am never at rest.
> I have no fixed course or home or village.
> I have no power, O God, to end my wanderings;
> My soul dances about like rice in a frying pan.
> Ages have passed in this way and I do not know how many
>   more await me.

I cannot end my course, for it begins again;
Only the ending of the world can set me free.
Who will finish this suffering of mine?
Who will take my burden on himself?
Thy name will carry me over the sea of this world,
Thou dost run to help the distressed.
Now run to me, *Narayana*,[20] to me, poor and
    wretched as I am.
Consider neither my merits nor my faults.
Tukaram implores thy mercy.

(*The Poems of Tukaram,* translated by Fraser, J.N., and
Marathe, K.B., Christian Literature Society, Madras,
1909, pp 114-15, revised.)

A number of thinkers and reformers from India in particular, and the English-speaking world in general, also had immense impact on developments in Jaffna, and many people were drawn into the reformist movements initiated by them. The writings of leading figures like Jeremy Bentham (1748-1832), Ram Mohan Roy (1774-1833), Karl Marx (1818-1883), Ramakrishna (1834-1886), Keshub Chunder Sen (1838-1884), Annie Besant (1847-1933), Rabindranath Tagore (1861-1941), Vivekananda (1862-1902), and Mahatma Gandhi (1869-1948) were read avidly, and a number of societies and organisations sprang up to promote the ideas, and ideals, put forward by such leaders.

But as Albert Schweitzer has pointed out, most of these reformers were influenced by western thought. That they "undertook more energetically than any of their predecessors to combine with the ethic of becoming more perfect of heart the ethic which seeks activity within the world is, of course, due to the fact that they had become acquainted with, and influenced by, modern European world and life affirmation and the Christian ethic of love. But this stimulus from without only set in motion a process of development which had already begun independently." Of Ram Mohan Roy, whom he described as "the great pioneer of modern Indian thought", Schweitzer observed:—

"Born of a Bengali Brahmin family, he devoted himself to research into all religions and was impressed by the personality and message of Jesus. In 1820 he published a book about his teaching (*The Precepts of Jesus*), which in his

---

20.   Lord Vishnu.

opinion contains ideas to which Indian thought does not ascribe sufficient importance ...

"In the year 1830 he went to England. His chief motive for the journey was that the law against widow-burning was in danger of being abrogated on account of the opposition organised against it by the Brahmins. During his stay he met Jeremy Bentham, the venerable but still fiery prophet of the rational love of mankind, and was saluted by him as 'an admired and beloved fellow-worker in the service of humanity.' He died on the 27th September 1833 at Bristol and lies buried there."[21]

Keshub Chunder Sen's affinity to Christ offended many of his followers, but his emphasis that Christ was the unique Son of God, and his message of the 'Asiatic Christ', for which India must be ready, attracted many followers. Quoting extensively from the New Testament, he pleaded for India to be ready to receive the 'bridegroom' and not to fall asleep like the 'foolish virgins.'

Ramakrishna's mission of love, humanity and universal brotherhood, as well as his philosophy of an all-embracing Godhead, appealed to millions throughout the world. Apart from organising several affiliated branches to propagate and practise Ramakrishna's ideals at grass-roots level, the Mission also played an active role in education by establishing and maintaining a number of schools in most parts of Ceylon, and contributed in no small measure to the moral, spiritual and social welfare of the people.

The charismatic leadership of Vivekananda, the chief disciple of Ramakrishna, gave the Mission a new momentum, in that it came to represent the consummation of religious thought at the dawn of the twentieth century. The all-embracing philosophy of a common world religion that Vivekananda preached, his charm and easy style of imparting his message, and his missionary zeal took the world by storm. Addressing the Parliament of Religions in Chicago in 1893, he spelt out his message in unmistakable terms:—

"... if there is ever to be a universal religion, it must be one which will have no location in place or time; which will be infinite, like the God it will preach, and whose sun will shine upon the followers of Krishna and of Christ, on saints and sinners alike; which will not be Brahmanic or Buddhistic, Christian or Mohammedan, but the sum-total of all these, and still have

---

21. Schweitzer, A., *Indian Thought and Its Development*, Adam and Charles Black, London, 1956, pp 209-11.

infinite space for development; which in its catholicity will embrace in its infinite arms, and find a place for, every human being....

"It will be a religion which will have no place for persecution or intolerance in its polity, which will recognise divinity in every man and woman, and whose whole scope, whose whole force, will be centred in aiding humanity to realize its own true, divine nature."[22]

This new message of hope and reconciliation reached many corners of the world, including Ceylon, where the reverberations are still very much alive.

As one of the most prestigious personalities of his generation, Rabindranath Tagore, too, attracted a large audience worldwide, including Jaffna, where many of his writings and poems found a ready reception, some being incorporated into school textbooks in both English and Tamil. The ethical world of life affirmation that he presented, combined with the message of a common humanity, reflecting the thoughts of some of the best thinkers of the western world like Shaftesbury, Kant and Fichte, excited the intellectual verve of Jaffna, especially following the award of the Nobel Prize for Literature to him in 1913.

Mahatma Gandhi, though, marked the final pinnacle of the intellectual fervour that gripped Jaffna, not only because of his political struggle for Indian independence, but also because he represented an ethical ideology immediately relevant to the common man and woman. By drawing freely from Western thought, from the New Testament, from Ruskin's *Unto This Last* and Tolstoy's *Kingdom of God is Within You*, and from the *Bhagavad Gita*, all of which, he confessed, had made a lasting impact on his thinking, he did touch many hearts and minds and usher in a new era of hope for mankind.

The Gandhian revolution set off an international momentum that had significant impact on Jaffna, where the emergent English-educated classes were flexing their muscles for greater adventures into the unknown than ever before in Jaffna's history. The most vociferous followers of Gandhi were teachers and senior students, representing diverse social and religious groups, most of them articulate with an adequate knowledge of English, and aware of social and political changes that were taking place elsewhere.

---

22. Vivekananda, D., *Complete Works*, Vol. 1, Prabuddha Bharata, Almora, Madras, 1919, pp 4 et seq.

The founding of the Students' Congress in 1924, later known as the Youth Congress, is a case in point. Jaffna College, founded by the American Ceylon Mission, became the focal point, where a number of undergraduates were reading for the External Degree examinations of the Universities of Madras and London. A young teacher, S. Handy-Perinbanayagam, a radical thinker, and graduate of the University of London with a sound knowledge of English, Latin, and socio-political developments, emerged as the undisputed leader of the upsurge of social conscience that manifested itself. He led from the front, to encompass, and contain, a cascade of escalating emotions. He set an example by discarding the western suit in favour of the national dress, and choosing a low caste boy to be his personal aid. When the Rev. John Bicknell, the Principal of Jaffna College, took the unprecedented step to admit low caste students to the College, all the teachers protested and showed their opposition by boycotting the classes, but 'Handy Master', as he was popularly known, stood by the Principal, to the extent that the students from the depressed communities were eventually allowed to have their meals with the rest of the students at the same table.

Ever since the first session of the Students' Congress in December, 1924, invitations had been extended to Mahatma Gandhi, some through personal contacts, to visit Jaffna and bless the youth movement in person. When at last it materialised on 29 November, 1927, there was euphoria, to say the least. A founder-member of the Congress described the mood:—

> "The goal we set before us was very high. We wished to know our minds on a few of the most urgent issues of our national life. We would devote our energies to the attainment of *Purna Swaraj*, which meant total political, social and economic emancipation for our country. We would herald in a cultural renaissance ..."[23]

Many members of the Youth Congress went on to make a mark in national life, especially in the field of education.

Of significance, too, was the publication of the *Eeela Kesari*, the first secular paper in Jaffna, in June 1930. Independent it might have been, but it was sympathetic to the cause of the Youth Congress and facilitated the articulation of a wide spectrum of public opinion. The name of the publication was also significant—*Eelam*, the name by which Ceylon, and in particular North Ceylon, was

---

23. Subramaniam, C., *Homage To A Guru*, Handy-Perinbanayagam Remembrance Committee, Jaffna, 1978, pp 12-13.

known in India, combined with *Kesari*, meaning 'Lion', the name of a paper in India at the time, campaigning for national independence.

Tamil Drama too underwent radical changes as a consequence of the impact of English, especially under the guidance and patronage of South Indian dramatists like *Padma Booshan* Rao Bahadur P. Sambanda Mudaliyar, the chief architect behind the success of the *Suguna Vilasa Sabah*, the leading dramatic group. As a matter of fact, *Kalai Arasu* K. Chornalingam of Jaffna, who acknowledged Sambanda Mudaliyar as his Guru, had visited South India on a number of occasions, mainly to meet his Guru and learn at his feet, as he put it to the present writer, the methods and practices used by his mentor to produce a number of successful and economically viable plays and stage them before appreciative audiences. With the inspiration that he received from his visits, Chornalingam was mainly instrumental in establishing the *Subhoda Vilasa Sabah* in Ceylon in 1913, modelled on the Indian prototype. The indigenous society produced and staged a number of plays successfully, including some popular plays of Shakespeare. It also staged a few plays brought down from India by the *Suguna Vilasa Sabah*, with Sambanda Mudaliyar playing some leading roles to the acclaim of excited audiences. Milton Singer explains the impact:—

> "The amateurs, particularly the *Suguna Vilasa Sabah*, undertook to stage a great variety of plays, *Kalidasa* in Sanskrit, Shakespeare in English, and plays in Tamil, Telugu, Canarese, and Hindi. They also occasionally took them to the country and to Ceylon. The professionals are more limited in scope. As in the cinema, which is the chief medium now for popular drama, the aim is to reach a wide audience, so Tamil is the major language."[24]

A substantial body of literature in Tamil was traditionally assigned between two major categories, pertaining to the Home or Home Front, and the Outside World, known as *Aham* and *Puram* respectively. While the former dealt with life, love and death including the internal terrain and its natural attributes, *Puram* was concerned with the external frontiers of life like acquisitions and conquests including battles and the war front. The latter category of literature was largely responsible for the sea-faring and industrious acumen for which Tamils came to be known, as well as their fighting and pioneering spirit. For example, a typical poem in *Puram* runs thus:—

---

24. Singer, M., *WHEN A GREAT TRADITION MODERNIZES*, op. cit., p 165.

You stand within the foyer
Of my house,
And impertinently ask
'Where's your son?'
You've left me flabbergasted!
For my womb
Was a provisional lair
For the cub;
Find him ... In the Battlefield!"

Purananooru, 87

The pioneering spirit of the Jaffna Tamils is well documented by Howard Wriggins. He writes:—

"The largest minority group are the Ceylon Tamils who represent 11 per cent of the total population. They are concentrated chiefly in the northern and eastern areas of the island. The city of Jaffna is still the principal center of their cultural and religious life. As a people, they are widely believed to be descendants of Tamils who came to Ceylon, in successive waves of immigration and military invasion, from Dravidian South India between A.D. 400 and 1200. Their language is the same as the Tamil spoken in South India, and they are Hindus. Life in northern and eastern provinces is hard and agricultural resources are limited by insufficient rains. The economic opportunities which came to the wet zone with the British tea and rubber estates did not affect the already overcrowded northern peninsula. Hence, Ceylon Tamils sought opportunity in all parts of the island, and especially in the larger cities such as Colombo and Kandy. Many Tamil families have lived there for generations but retain family connections with Jaffna. Ceylon Tamils even went as far afield as Malaya and Singapore in search of new employment."[25]

No doubt, the impetus given by English education gave Jaffna an enviable edge, and large numbers of Tamils moved to other parts of the country, as well as

---

25. Wriggins, W.H., *CEYLON—Dilemmas of a New Nation*, Princeton, New Jersey, 1960, pp 22-23.

abroad. S.A. Pakeman who spent more than thirty years in Ceylon in the higher echelons of the administrative service did aptly observe:

> "The Tamils had taken to English rather more thoroughly, in the Northern Province and elsewhere, and had obtained posts in the government service far in excess of their proportion of the population; it has been jestingly said that Government service was the principal industry in Jaffna."[26]

It is, therefore, not coincidental that a wit of the time is said to have quipped: "The father is making hay in Jaffna, while the son is shining in Colombo!"

There were far-reaching ramifications, too. When the British administration in Malaya and Singapore needed English educated personnel to run the essential services during the early years of British rule, they turned to the Government of Ceylon, and naturally many Tamils took advantage of the new opportunities that were opening up. The *Malay Mail* reported exactly a hundred years ago:—

> "*The Times of Ceylon* calls attention to the steady increase in the emigration of Tamils from Jaffna in that island to the Federated Malay States. Last year 1000 Jaffnese, who are called the Scotsmen of the East, left Colombo for the Straits Settlements and the Federated Malay States. They were mostly young men going in search of employment, the next largest representing the wives and children of those who had gone and found a home for their families in the Straits. It is reported that the young Jaffna Tamil gravitates to the Post Offices and clerkships in the Straits and that he is a strong rival to the young Malay who is said to write a 'copper plate hand' when copying letters etc. From all accounts reaching Ceylon, the young Jaffnese are doing well out further East and some of them have risen to positions of trust and responsibility in the Straits."[27]

The more sophisticated *Straits Times,* however, commenting three decades later, demonstrated a lot more perspicacity when it wrote:—

> "The close link between Malaya and Ceylon in the early days was commented on by Sir Malcolm Watson in Colombo a few days ago. 'In some ways Malaya may be regarded as a colony of Ceylon', he said. When the British entered Malaya in the 'seventies on account of the disturbances, it was to Ceylon that the British Government turned for people to organize a just

---

26. Pakeman, S.A., *CEYLON*, Earnest Benn, London, 1964, p 181.
27. *Malay Mail,* 13 February, 1906.

administration in Malaya. We sent to Ceylon for Public Works Department Engineers and to this day the staff of the P.W.D. consists largely of men from Ceylon. In the same way the staff of the Railways was largely Ceylonese. The Posts and Telegraphs and Medical Departments were again manned by people from the Island."[28]

When a Jaffna Tamil was elevated to the position of Malaya's first High Commissioner to India in 1957, the *Singapore Standard* commented editorially under the heading 'Ceylon Tamils':—

"The Federation Government has conferred a signal honour on the Ceylon Tamil community in this country by appointing Mr. S. Chelvasingam MacIntyre of Batu Pahat as Malaya's first High Commissioner to India. The Ceylon Tamils, or Jaffnese as they are known in this country, have been connected with the civil service for many decades. At one time they held most of the posts in Government Departments, particularly the Malayan Railway. Even today they are strongly represented in the public services ...

"Many Jaffnese have made their mark in this country. They possess one outstanding trait in a land of free spenders—thrift. To their credit they saved millions of dollars out of their salaries much of which have been sent home to Jaffna. Yet quite a good percentage of these savings are kept in Malaya, as witness the strong financial position of their Co-operative Societies. Before the war they founded in Kuala Lumpur the Bank of Jaffna ..."[29]

A closer look reveals that those who went to Malaya and Singapore in the first few waves of migration were indeed 'Pioneers' in the real sense of the term. They went alone leaving their families behind, risking their lives as well as the future livelihood of their dependants. Sir George Maxwell, K.B.E., C.M.G., a distinguished civil servant whose family had served in Malaya for about three generations, summed up the spirit of those early pioneers when he wrote:—

"On more than one occasion in speeches which have not been reported, I have referred to the great debt which Malaya owes to the Jaffnese. People come and go in Malaya and the present generation cannot realise the circumstances in which the last generation lived and worked. For the first twenty or twenty five years, after the introduction of British protection into the Malay States, there were very few really educated Chinese, and particularly no

---

28. *Straits Times*, 4 December, 1937.
29. *Singapore Standard*, 29 August, 1957.

locally educated Malays, who were competent to fill in the Government Service appointments without which the Government would not be administered. The Government, in fact, was dependent on the Jaffnese. In the early days a new arrival from Jaffna would, with true courage, proceed perhaps immediately after his arrival in a strange country, to take up work, far away in the jungle, in connection with some road or railway construction work which the men born and bred in the country would refuse to accept. Throughout the Malay States, there are lonely graves of these men of the early days, and of men too of our times."[30]

On retirement, many chose to return to Jaffna with their enhanced pensions and invaluable experience, and contributed in very large measure to the development of their homeland.

---

30.   Maxwell, Sir George, The Mixed Communities of Malaya, *British Malaya*, February, 1943, pp 115 et seq.

4

SOCIO-ECONOMIC

Village life in general was determined and often prescribed by an intricate web of rights, responsibilities and obligations, not only within one's immediate family, including the extended or joint family, but also the community at large.

There is evidence to suggest that the Tamils, like the Japanese, are an achievement-oriented people whose motivation springs from the mutually supportive system of social relationships, beginning with duties, responsibilities and obligations within the family, and gradually extending beyond.[1]

Being a maritime people both in peninsular India and North Ceylon, the Tamils took to the sea from very early times, and as a consequence developed a universality of outlook. For instance, one of the early poets sang:—

> Every town's my home town,
> Every hamlet home;
> Everyone my kinsman,
> All folk kith and kin.
>
> Kanniyan Punkunran

The village was naturally the basic economic unit and subsistence agriculture, fishing and minimal commercial transactions the basic economic activities. Such economic activities as practised were largely associated with the institutions of caste, land tenure and joint family. Rice was cultivated in smallholdings and familial relationships as well as the need for security necessitated the concentration of compact communities in small hamlets. As long as economic output could satisfy demand, such an arrangement proved advantageous. However, with increasing population and demand, there was the need for the institutions to

---

1. George, De Vos, A., Achievement Orientation, Social Self-Identity and Japanese Economic Growth, *Asian Survey*, Berkeley, December, 1965, pp 575 et seq.

adapt. It gave rise to a system of land tenure known as the *Varakudy* system, *varakudy* being the tenant who worked for the land-owning farmer. In other words, the tenants or agricultural labourers or serfs sold their services to the farmer, in view of their socio-economic circumstances, and in return, the farmer undertook to look after them. This form of land tenure, although enjoined by tradition and custom, was on the whole heavily loaded against the poor and the depressed, to the extent that sons were held responsible for their fathers' debts—a form of 'Bonded Labour'.

Land ownership being associated with social status, land values in Jaffna have been comparatively high, far in excess of their economic potential. Very few farmers could therefore own their land, and those who could had to be content with smallholdings averaging less than three-fourths of an acre. Whether it was the farmer who owned his small plot or the tenant who worked for the farmer, their greatest need was capital. The land-owning farmer had to resort to intensive cultivation to make ends meet, through a system of rotation of crops. It involved capital outlay towards seed, manure and fertilisers, intensive irrigation, and labour, including the use of cattle. The tenant would have needed capital to provide for the increasing demands of the family over and above the support extended by the farmer, to pay off the debts accrued during and/or before his tenancy, and perhaps to buy a small plot for himself. Credit was also needed for other purposes such as litigation, very common due to disputes arising from unregistered titles to property, and above all, expenses connected with social obligations in respect of marriages, funerals and ceremonies associated with religion, custom or tradition.

The usual sources of credit were the professional moneylenders and the traders cum middlemen. Moneylenders gave credit on adequate security such as valuable jewellery or property, movable as well as immovable, but usually only part of the real value of the items surrendered as security was given as loan, and the interest rates were usually exorbitant. The trader was a popular source of credit to the average farmer. He usually met three immediate needs, namely the supply of consumer goods on credit, provision of intermediary cash in advance of credit, and where necessary, the marketing of the produce on behalf of the farmer. Invariably, because of the inability of farmers to raise the necessary capital that was required at the outset, they had to depend on middlemen at all stages from planting to marketing. The middlemen had to charge exceptionally high rates of interest on the advances they paid to the farmers, because of the high risk they were taking. Immediately after harvest they bought the entire produce themselves at a price far below the market price, so that they could take advantage of fluctuating conditions. Such large-scale exploitation of labour by middlemen was all too common in Jaffna, not only in respect of agricultural produce, but also in other economic activities such as fishing.

In the absence of organised credit institutions, the problems faced by the small producers were almost insurmountable. In many cases it would not have been possible for them to borrow the amounts they actually needed. On the other hand, it would have been possible for some to borrow far in excess of their needs and their ability to repay. Also, the lender could lend at any time, but the farmer had to borrow at certain periods when his needs were greater than the needs of the lender to lend. This necessarily placed the farmer at a rather disadvantageous position, which led to exploitation, to the extent that the borrower would often be unaware of what he was committing himself to. In short, unorganised credit reduced the borrower to a state of helplessness, even subservience, servitude or bondage.

It was estimated that in 1951 thirty per cent of rural families in Ceylon were in debt and the average debt per family was Rs.263. By 1957, fifty four per cent of rural families were in debt and the average debt per family had increased to Rs.750. It was also found that in most cases the debts were incurred for non-productive purposes at very high rates of interest, and that over ninety per cent of the loans were obtained from private money-lenders.[2] In fact, the All India Rural Credit Survey of 1954 had already demonstrated that moneylenders met about 70 per cent of the credit requirements of farmers.[3] A subsequent survey in 1967-68 in North-East Bihar too confirmed the above finding.[4]

As in many developing countries, far too much dependence on the Government to solve all problems, mostly in the economic field, has been the main obstacle to development in Ceylon. W. K. H. Campbell, a former Registrar of Co-operative Societies in Ceylon who earned the respect of many officials in the Co-operative sector for his dedicated service, did observe that "the inhabitants tend to be resigned and apathetic, mistrustful of their own abilities, disinclined to exert

2.   Tilakaratne, W.M., Problem of Rural Credit in Ceylon, *Ceylon Co-operative Review*, Vol.1, No.1, March, 1967, pp 6 et seq.

3.   Reserve Bank of India, *All India Rural Credit Survey*, Vol.11, Bombay, 1954, p 167.

4.   Ladejinsky, W., Green Revolution in Bihar—The Kosi Area: A Field Trip, *Economic and Political Weekly, Review of Agriculture*, (India), September, 1969, p 152.

themselves and apt to assume that the initiation of all action is the business of the government."[5]

In regard to the extended family, Bauer and Yamey had pointed out:—

> "On the negative side it acts as a serious obstacle to economic progress. A man is much less likely to be willing and able to rise in the income scale, and to save and invest, when he knows that, should he succeed in improving his position, he would have to maintain a large number of distant relatives ... At the same time the system, which is largely indiscriminate in its operation, minimises the inducement for people to improve their own position because they can count on being provided with the means of subsistence at a level not very different from that of the majority of their kinsmen, including the more energetic, thrifty and able. The system has other adverse effects which are less obvious."[6]

In a scathing attack on entrenched attitudes and values in most developing countries, Thomas Balogh writes of the shameful imitation of the expatriate mode of living by the new African (and, to a lesser extent, Asian) governmental, civil service, and commercial elites, which has brought about a class apartheid to a degree hardly equalled even by very old-fashioned imperial expatriates. He goes on to explain that the shortage of skilled manpower, especially in "the vital rural sector" is "an interesting consequence of poverty, but also of tribal, feudal or religious attitudes which are incompatible with collective and individual social responsibility, cohesion and economic incentives ..." Balogh concludes that the "suggestion that education should be modelled consciously to serve the task of social transformation and adapted to the means and needs of the less developed world was as repugnant to the *bien-pensant* as it was to the privileged, exploiting the national revulsion against foreign domination for the protection of their own advantage. The actual history of de-colonisation has in most cases resulted in the rise of a new elite, which is as hostile to change in this respect as had been their predecessors and adversaries. Once more it has been shown that no vested interest is as dangerous and ferocious as that of the intellect."[7]

---

5.   Campbell, W.K.H., *Practical Co-operation in Asia and Africa*, W. Heffer and Sons, Cambridge, 1951, p 10.
6.   Bauer, P.T., and Yamey, B.S., *The Economics of Under-Developed Countries*, Nisbett and Sons, Cambridge, 1957 (Reprinted 1963), p 66.
7.   Balogh, T., *The Economics of Poverty*, Weidenfeld and Nicolson, London, 1974, pp 5, 24, and 39 et seq.

In fact, the new elites or bureaucrats in independent Sri Lanka came to be referred to by prominent journalists like Tarzie Vittachi as 'Brown Sahibs', i.e., 'dark-skinned elites' who replaced their white counterparts. They have been, on the whole, responsible for the slow developmental pace in the country since independence, giving rise to a whole host of rules and regulations accompanied by mountains of forms that needed to be filled in before the ordinary citizen could even catch a glimpse of the 'brown' master to make his or her representation.

The more rigid the caste system the more behaviour, mental states and attitudes are determined by group sanctions rather than by private conscience or individual decision. Max Weber had looked at the many sociological aspects of the Hindu caste system. Firstly, in spite of all efforts to fight caste segregation in industry and commerce, he had come across many instances of resistance, mostly psychological, from those segregated against. The reasons are not far to seek. Particular crafts, in so far as they are the preserves of particular castes, are assigned a religious sanction and given the character of a sacred vocation. Thus, he observes, "each caste nourishes its feeling of worth by its technically expert execution of its assigned vocation."

Secondly, the idea of karma and the belief in transmigration arose from the conviction that any likelihood of one improving one's chances in subsequent incarnations depended on the faithful execution of one's vocation assigned one by God, and any attempt to intrude into the sphere of activities assigned to other caste groups as well as higher castes, would end in disaster, and possibly result in unfavourable incarnation in the future. Weber explains:—

> "It is precisely the lowest classes, who would naturally be most desirous of improving their status in subsequent incarnations, that cling most steadfastly to their caste obligations, never thinking of toppling the caste system through social revolutions or reforms. Among the Hindus, the Biblical emphasis echoed in Luther's injunction 'Remain steadfast in your vocation', was elevated into a cardinal religious obligation and was fortified by powerful religious sanctions."

He went on to add:—

> "… the more depressed the position in which the members of the pariah people found themselves, the more closely did the religion cause them to cling to one another and to their pariah position and the more powerful

became the salvation hopes which were connected with the divinely ordered fulfilment of their religious obligations."[8]

Talcott Parsons in his Introduction to Weber's *Sociology of Religion* observed:

"On the oriental side, Hinduism has been a kind of Indian Catholicism. It mitigated the severity of the pure Buddhist-type doctrine by supplementing it with a social sacramentalism ..."[9]

Culture does not merely encompass values or personality types or attitudes, but rather an entire corpus of inherited knowledge and intelligence, ideals and aspirations, as well as models and techniques of socio-economic organisation for survival in a competitive environment. Values ascribed to particular religions and cultures as inhibiting development have come under scrutiny by a succession of sociologists and developmental economists since the largely ideological theories in the tradition of Max Weber came into vogue early in the twentieth century. Jeffrey Sachs is, perhaps, the first economist to mount some constructive arguments questioning the validity of such theories.

They "tried to explain," he writes, "the lower incomes of Southern Europe and Ireland relative to Northern Europe on the basis of supposedly static values of Catholicism versus entrepreneurial values of Protestantism. After mid-century, the Catholic countries began to grow very rapidly, especially after malaria was controlled. By now, Catholic Italy and Ireland have overtaken the Protestant UK in per capita income. Similarly, Weber and his followers hypothesized that East Asian societies with Confucian values, notably China, would be unable to achieve economic progress. Later, when China and other countries of East Asia began to grow rapidly," Asian values "were invoked as the explanation for success, turning the argument on its head. When Asia had a temporary economic crisis in 1997, Asian values were once again attacked as the culprit, but this interpretation quickly faded when economic recovery came a couple of years later. India's poverty was explained on the basis of Hindu social rigidities and mysticism, until of course, India became one of the fastest growing economies in the world in the 1990s.

---

8.   Weber, Max, *The Sociology of Religion*, Methuen, London, 1966, pp 41-43; 109 et seq.

9.   Ibid., p liii.

"In the wake of September 11, Islamic societies have been categorized by some Western observers to be unfit for modernity. The charges of cultural failure are legion: irrationality, fundamentalism, extreme bias against women, antipathy to science. Yet some of the fastest growing economies in the world in the past decade have been Islamic ..." Culture-based predictions, he argues, "are fragile and often incorrect even in the most culture-bound areas of human behaviour," because "cultural arguments hold two main problems. Most important, cultures change with economic times and circumstances ... The second main problem with cultural interpretations is that they are usually made on the basis of prejudice rather than measurable evidence. The arguments tend to be circular ..."[10]

Bert F. Hoselitz spoke of "environmental conditions" for economic growth which, he thought, ought to be sought mainly in the non-economic aspects of a society, for, in his view, "economic growth is a process which affects not only purely economic relations but the entire social, political, and cultural fabric of a society."[11]

Provision of irrigation facilities and encouragement of cooperatives for sugar production were two of the strategies adopted for agricultural development in Maharashtra, India, following the recommendations of the Famine Commission (1901) and the Irrigation Commission (1903). The two dominant social groups in Maharashtra responded differently to the new economic opportunities that opened up. The different responses were not only the result of different economic circumstances of the two groups, but also how the groups perceived themselves and their long-term interests in the light of their own values and attitudes.

The Malis were the first to see the benefits that the irrigation canals would bring them. In this they were helped by their natural resources and their values and attitudes. They had the necessary experience and expertise in irrigation farming, access to capital, willingness to change over from subsistence to commercial farming, and the capacity and will to migrate if necessary. The Marathas, the other dominant group, viewed the new opportunities differently. Reluctant at the start, they were rather slow in adapting to the changes that the provision of irrigation facilities involved. Therefore, the majority were content to hand over their farms

---

10. Sachs, J. D., *The End of Poverty*, Penguin Books, London, 2005, pp 316-17.
11. Hoselitz, B.F., Non-Economic Factors in Economic Development, *American Economic Review—Papers and Proceedings*, May, 1957, pp 28-41.

to the Malis at low rents, the poorer among them even prepared to work as labourers on the sugar farms managed by the Malis.

In the development of cooperative sugar factories, the Marathas were more enthusiastic than the Malis. They no doubt perceived that the new cooperatives would strengthen their position vis-à-vis the other groups, whereas the Malis and others were apprehensive of the effect the cooperatives would have on the relative balance of power between the different caste groups.[12]

The above study, while recognising that any analysis of social situations that ignores cultural factors would be superficial, illustrates that good timing is also important. Opportunities are there to be grasped and history is littered with those taken with open arms to the betterment of peoples' livelihoods, and those squandered in the maelstrom of conflict of interests.

Writing in 1975, a Special Rapporteur of the United Nations Commission on Human Rights observed in the context of both India and Ceylon:—

"Throughout the region, the response of the diverse groups and social classes to modern values and institutions has varied greatly, and this, in turn, has been one of the most important bases for new lines of social stratification. Generally speaking, as the rulers of India prior to the British, the Muslims proved more resistant to Western values and education than the Hindus. The *kayasthas, boidyas* and *brahmans* in Bengal responded earlier than did other castes in their localities. Tamil-speaking people along the Madras coast responded more rapidly than the interior Telugus, the Bengalis more than the Biharis or Oriyas, the Punjabi and Uttar Pradesh Muslims before other Muslims."[13]

Although caste, like other traditional institutions, has been subject to changes as a result of education, social mobility, urbanisation and more enlightened public perceptions, it has nevertheless continued to intensify existing divisions by substituting new lines of social stratification. The U N Special Rapporteur quoted above also went on to comment that "Political independence, together with industrialisation, secularisation and education have all worked towards a new

---

12.   Baviskar, B. S., Opportunity and Response: Social Factors in Agricultural Development in Maharashtra, *IDS Bulletin*, Vol.8, No.2, September, 1976, University of Sussex, pp 22-26.

13.   Ganji, M., *The Realization of Economic, Social and Cultural Rights:Problems, Policies, Progress*, U.N., New York, 1975, pp 110-11.

social stratification. What Bryce Ryan wrote on the changing character of caste in Ceylon in the 1950s was also true of India:

"'The revolution which is pervading all Ceylonese institutions cannot leave caste untouched, for caste is a phenomenon integrated with feudal, person-alised, and familial status relationships. Neither the values nor the structure of a secular and economically rational democratic state and economy can support this institution of another era. Many specific trends encompassed in the Ceylonese transformation operate to disrupt the caste system directly, as well as to shatter the social order which supports it. The widening popular, and virtually complete legal, acceptance of equality in opportunity and jus-tice, and belief in the propriety of status by achievement bespeak a value sys-tem explicitly contradictory to caste. The joint development of urbanism and economic rationality, with their combined effects on mobility, the growth of contractual relations and impersonality, provide objective circum-stances in which structures of caste are unenforceable. Even more signifi-cantly, they establish disparities between traditional birth statuses and economic prestige and power.'(Ryan, Bryce, *Caste in Modern Ceylon*, New Brunswick, 1953, p.338.)

"Nevertheless, the growth of new classes in administration, commerce and industry on the basis of education and economic status has intensified existing divisions along lines of religion, language and caste and thereby exacerbated group conflict in the various communities."[14]

Howard Wriggins did, however, point out that:—

"In the Tamil Hindu areas of Ceylon, caste stratifications are clearer and the position of the upper cultivator caste—the *Vellala*—has not yet been chal-lenged, either by modern economic conditions or by other caste-conscious groups."[15]

The point that needs to be underscored is that the new class divisions have inten-sified erstwhile differences and exacerbated group conflict, to the detriment of unhindered economic development.

---

14. Ibid.
15. Wriggins, W.H., *Ceylon—Dilemmas of a New Nation*, op. cit., p 25.

Van Wengen recorded three years before Wriggins:—

> "In a small village near Jaffna an informal discussion was in progress between the head of the co-operative department in the northern province and members of the local credit society. Among the representatives of the society were two members of the lowest caste. During the discussion which took place in the private house of one of the board members of the cooperative society, these two were compelled to sit outside, because in this particular community their presence in the house of a man of higher caste was not permitted."[16]

The above incident as reported has many implications and interpretations. Apart from the manifestation of a sharp social gulf between the caste groups, the important lesson seems to be that the head of the co-operative department in the province and the vast majority of the members of that particular society, obviously from the higher castes, decided to conduct their deliberations concerning the cooperative at the private residence of one of the members, to the exclusion of two members of the lower caste, the latter being 'compelled to sit outside', because 'their presence in the house of a man of higher caste was not permitted.' In other words, the two who were excluded compulsorily had no choice whatsoever in the matter, which amounted to a defiance of the basic philosophy and principles of the Co-operative Movement. Secondly, it gives a clue to where the leadership came from, and how the officials and the members who ran the cooperatives invariably came from the upper castes and imposed on those below them a kind of benevolent paternalism.

There is yet another side of the same coin that cannot be overlooked. It seems that the two members, openly and deliberately discriminated against, did not wish to disturb the status quo, but instead acquiesced, in order to safeguard their immediate interests, by overlooking what amounted to be discrimination against them on grounds of caste inferiority, and even humiliation. It also appears that, perhaps, they did not wish to inflict any damage to the socio-religious equilibrium in the long term for fear of interfering with what was pre-determined for them in the after-life!

Perhaps Max Weber was smiling in his grave, after all!!

---

16. Van Wengen, G.D., *Social Aspects of the Co-operative Movement in Ceylon and Southern India*, DICO, Amsterdam, 1957, p 24.

5

POLITICAL

The Colebrooke-Cameron Recommendations for Reform (1832), far in advance of the time in colonial perspective, consequently had far-reaching implications for the rest of the colonial administration. However, as the local bureaucrats obviously lacked the vision that was implicit in the major recommendations, for "more than a decade following the publication of the reports of Colebrooke and Cameron, Ceylon was in the doldrums."[1] The fact of the matter is that Colebrooke's recommendations regarding the administration and finance were as radical and far-reaching as Cameron's proposals for judicial reform. Their aim in the end was to bring about Social Justice based on sound ethical principles, but it was perhaps too much for the bureaucrats to digest. The result was, as to be expected, catastrophic. The franchise was not extended until 1931, that is, a hundred years after the Colebrooke-Cameron Recommendations specifically in that respect. Although the principle of local participation in the country's government was accepted by 1920 and the first Legislative Council came into being in 1921 with a very limited franchise, four per cent of the population, the overriding powers given to the Council's Official Members, had the inevitable result of watering down the political significance of the Legislative Council.

The Legislative Council gave way to the State Council in 1931, when for the first time in the country's history, elections to the Council based on the principle of universal franchise were held. Yet out of a total membership of 61, 50 were elected, 8 nominated, and 3 were Officers-of-State appointed by the Governor. Although the State Council could choose its Board of Ministers, the Governor had the ultimate power of the veto. In retrospect, perhaps it was a precautionary measure, given the apathy of the general public towards political freedom and responsibility. As it happened, seventeen years later, rather unwittingly and ill-prepared, Ceylon was granted independence along with Burma as a matter of

---

1.   Bailey, S.D., *CEYLON*, op. cit., p 101.

course, perhaps exigency, following the liberation of India which had to endure long and protracted negotiations, not to mention the many humiliating and bitter struggles, before independence became a reality. Ceylon and Burma, like Pakistan (and its offshoot Bangladesh) before them, are still grappling with the thorny problem of constitutional reform.

However, in any agitation for political reform in Ceylon, it was the English educated who took the lead, and Jaffna was inevitably in the forefront. Howard Wriggins puts the picture in perspective:—

"... The Jaffna Peninsula is an area of highly concentrated population, equipped with good schools, and a literate and hard working population. Its concentration lends itself to intensive political organisation, unlike the eastern and Sinhalese areas outside Western province. Professional associations of lawyers, school and college teachers, and doctors have been the principal articulators of political demands ..."[2]

Power continued to be concentrated in the hands of the elites, however, based on traditional institutional loyalties. Howard Wriggins explains again:—

"Ceylon is a plural society, a mosaic of self-aware communities distinguished from one another along ethnic, religious, or linguistic grounds. Lacking strong parties derived from disciplined organisation, from clear-cut economic or revolutionary differences, or from an intense struggle for independence, Ceylon's political life has been closely bound up with these communal and other traditional social differentiations. Until now, these traditional groupings have formed the basis of most politically significant loyalties, interests, and demands. As local political leaders have responded to the imperatives of representative politics, these differences have often been played upon and accentuated. Loyalty is still directed to the extended family, clan, or to the caste, racial, religious, or linguistic group. An island-wide national sense is yet to be effectively evolved."[3]

As a direct consequence of the lackadaisical approach to constitutional reform, both on the part of the government and the general public, a highly centralised politico-administrative machinery reminiscent of colonial days continued to survive well into the latter half of the twentieth century; so much so that more than

---

2.   Wriggins, W.H., *Ceylon—Dilemmas of a New Nation*, op. cit., p 143.
3.   Ibid., p 20.

twenty years on since independence it was observed by an international and independent team of experts that "the system remained a set of highly centralised,
semi-autonomous departments, partially co-ordinated at the centre by the power
of the budget and co-ordinated locally in some degree by government agents (22
in number) and divisional revenue officers (150 in number)."[4]

Apart from the general apathy and inertia that such a centralised form of government promoted, it led to the emergence of the politician as the central crucial figure in the life of the people, with the inevitable consequences of bribery and
corruption, and nepotism at all levels of public administration. It meant that a
fertile ground was made available for various malcontent, dissident and chauvinistic groups who had been lurking in the background for years to emerge, and
with the able assistance of those political leaders to whom they owed allegiance,
make their voices heard. For instance, the move to make Sinhala and Tamil the
official languages to replace English was already being mooted in the State Council long before independence, and after much deliberation, accepted almost
unanimously. Yet, in the eight years following independence, there was such a
radical shift of public opinion, and consequently, political will, that the Official
Languages Act of 1956 making Sinhala the only Official Language was passed by
a majority of 65 against 28! In such a diabolical move that was viewed as nothing
short of an insult to the Tamil-speaking minority, not the slightest effort was
made at least to temper the cold wind with a biting edge to it, for the shorn
Tamil lamb. Already the disenfranchisement of a large proportion of the Tamil-
speaking population in the Tea and Rubber plantations through the Citizenship
Acts[5] had weakened the effectiveness of the Tamil voice in national affairs, and a
host of laws, rules and regulations that followed suit sought to ensure that Ceylon
was headed towards a 'Divided Nation.'

Indeed, in his Foreword to *Ceylon—A Divided Nation* by B.H. Farmer, Lord
Soulbury, the Chairman of the Commission on the Constitution for Independent Ceylon, quoted the observations of Sir Charles Jefferies in his book *Ceylon—the Path to Independence*, viz. "The Soulbury Constitution had entrenched
in it all the protective provisions for minorities that the wit of man could devise.
Nevertheless in the light of later happenings, I now think it is a pity that the

---

4. *Matching Employment Opportunities and Expectations—A Programme of Action for
    Ceylon*, ILO, Geneva, 1971, p 149.
5. Ceylon Citizenship Act, 1948; Emigrants Act, 1948; Indian and Pakistani Residents
    Act, 1949; Elections Amendment Act, 1949.

Commission did not also recommend the entrenchment in the Constitution, guarantees of fundamental rights, on the lines enacted in the constitutions of India, Pakistan, Malaya, Nigeria and elsewhere …"[6] Farmer himself, in the Introduction to his book, bemoaned the fact that the "Island Without Problems", which had been held up as a model for all the world, could no longer be regarded as such.

Walter Schwarz summed up the frustration not only of the Tamil speaking people of Ceylon but all those interested in good governance, when he observed:—

> "The Tamil problem is a classic case of a minority emerging at a heavy disadvantage from the relative impartiality of a colonial regime to the hazards of electioneering and demagogic democracy—a head count in which they must always lose."[7]

The mere process of how people vote, and those elected as representatives speak for the people in any legislature, are both vital ingredients of the democratic idea. Nevertheless, while democracy is an idea, it is also at the same time a machinery, and a democracy dependent on a faulty machinery is for all intents and purposes itself faulty.

When Sir Charles Jefferies clearly exonerates Lord Soulbury and his cohorts, as seen above, by observing that "The Soulbury Constitution had entrenched in it all the protective provisions for minorities that the wit of man could devise," it is nothing short of a hyperbole in the light of all the events that ensued, including the unprecedented communal riots and bloodletting of 1958. As the present writer recalls, "Have the Sinhalese and Tamils reached the parting of the ways?" was the rhetorical question with which Tarzie Vittachi concluded his journalistic masterpiece *Emergency '58* (Andre Deutsch, 1958).

The Soulbury Commission had very limited time to study the deep-seated problems that had plagued the nation for a very long time. The Commission was in the country for barely six months, in fact from December 1944 to April 1945, and their recommendations were to a great extent influenced by the proposals before the Secretary of State by early 1944. No doubt the most significant of all the proposals submitted to the Commission was the plea by the Tamil represen-

---

6.   Farmer, B.H., *Ceylon—A Divided Nation*, Oxford University Press, 1963, p 9.

7.   Schwarz, W., *The Tamils of Sri Lanka*, Minority Rights Group Report, No.25, London, 1975, p 7.

tatives for 'balanced representation', which came to be deliberately misrepresented as the 'Fifty-fifty Scheme'. The proposal by the Tamils was not in any way intended to interfere with the constitutional reforms advanced by the ministers, but was in the main intended to be a safeguard against one community gaining a dominant position in the government by virtue of sheer majority—to guard against the very untenable situation that Walter Schwarz was quick to point out in the Minority Rights Group Report of 1975, to which reference was made earlier. The so-called 'Fifty-fifty Scheme' was not arguing for a fifty percent stake in the government for Tamil representatives, as mischievously played upon by the government of the day and the media, but reiterating the rights of all the different minority groups to be represented. The proposal was unfortunately rejected by the Commission and the country has had to live with the consequences of political expediency and experimentation ever since. It would be wrong to suggest, however, that the members of the Soulbury Commission did not try, although subsequent developments clearly demonstrated that they did not try their best, especially given the subsequent parochial nature of political representation. For instance, the idea of proportional representation in some degree was the brainchild of the Commission itself, albeit at the instigation of the British Government. While the House of Representatives or Lower House was elected under the single-member district system, the Senate or Upper House was partly chosen by proportional representation. That is, whereas 15 out of the 30 members of the Senate were appointed by the Governor, the remaining 15 were chosen by proportional representation, using the single transferable vote. It must be pointed out, however, that neither the idea of a second chamber nor the inspiration for adopting some form of proportional representation came from the elected representatives themselves.

There is consensus among many thinkers and statesmen that democracy means much more than majority rule. Its basic component, they point out, is respect for individual as well as human rights. In other words, a democracy based on an unlimited and overwhelming majority would be as unjust and tyrannical as a dictatorship, for, the absence of any kind of limitations on an absolute and demagogic majority rule would be tantamount to a violation of an essential ingredient of democracy—the basic rights of the individual. It also questions the assumption that a mere 'representation' of dominant social groups in government would solve any political problem.

The Report of the Soulbury Commission which accorded substantially with the proposals put forward by the ministers in 1944 was published in September

1945. The consequences for the country were disastrous, to say the least. Apart from the phenomenon of dominant social groups who exploited and were in turn exploited by the emerging politicians, there was the traditional grip of the Buddhist clergy, the *Sangha*, on society in general and the politicians in government in particular. Casting his glance on the historical role of the clergy, the well-known archaeologist and historian, S. Paranavitana, comments:—

> "It is in keeping with the history of all similar civilisations of a despotic character and dependent on forced labour for the maintenance of large irrigation works on which their prosperity depended that the institutional machinery in time weakens and breaks down from obvious internal causes, let alone the invasions which plagued Raja Rata. While these latter may occasionally have served to rally national feeling and infuse new vigour, their cumulative effect must have been destructive, especially as they were accompanied or followed by renewed outbreaks of the internal dissension which has harried and drained Ceylon through most of its history. These forces must progressively have eaten away at the basic fabric of a state and society already losing its vigour with age. One would not expect evidence of this in the chronicles or inscriptions, given their nature and purpose. However, a fragmentary inscription on a slab of rock at the main anicut on the Mahaweli describing the Kalinga invasion of A.D.1210 reads in part as follows:
>
> "'The great host of Tamils descended on this Lanka, destroyed the Minister named Ati, and unhampered in all mountain fastnesses and forest fastnesses, swept over the whole of Lanka in the manner of the world-consuming flames at the end of an aeon, having destroyed the entire social structure and the religious organisation.'"[8]

With regard to Paranavitana's subsequent observation that on "the tillers of the soil rested the burden of supporting everyone else, divine as well as human, in addition to themselves", Ludowyk comments that "it is hard not to infer that the peasant staggering under a load too much for him symbolized the fortunes of the Sinhala kingdom."[9]

Kalinga invasions were not confined to Ceylon, although they resulted in violent upheavals in the country due to organised resistance by the rulers aided by the

---

8.   Paranavavitana, S., *Epigraphica Zelanica*, Vol. 5, Colombo, 1955, p 160.
9.   Ludowyk, E.F.C., *The Story of Ceylon*, op. cit., p 80.

laity and the clergy. In *The Story of Malaya,* W.S. Morgan of the Malayan Educational Service observed:—

> "In Europe men have always greatly prized the products of the East, and profits have been large to traders who have brought them—spices such as cinnamon, cloves, nutmeg and pepper to make food tastier, gold and silver, ivory and pearls to be used as ornaments, sweet-smelling woods such as sandalwood, drugs for medicines, and silks, thin muslins and cotton to make beautiful clothing. Traders from the Mediterranean, Phoenicians and Greeks, themselves came east for these goods, but the greatest traders between the East and West were Indians.
>
> "In southern India along the eastern coast was a land called *Tamilakam,* or the land of the Tamils. Forests shut it off from the rest of India, and it looked out to the sea. It was rich and civilised. There were harbours, and the forests gave good timber for making ships. So the Tamils naturally took to the sea and became sailors. From early times an eastern name for the people of this coast has been *Paradavar*, which means sailors."

Having observed that those sailors also went further east to the Malayan archipelago, East Indies and China to trade in articles such as silk, porcelain and gold, Morgan made the most significant contribution to an understanding of history when he made the observation that:

> "These Tamils, or Klings as they were called, for one of the kingdoms of *Tamilakam* was Kalinga, brought with them the ways and thoughts of their homeland, where in the cities and villages of the river deltas men led lives far more advanced than the simple fishing and hunting lives of the natives of the land where they settled. The result was like a fertiliser which enriches the soil …"[10]

The reader might wonder what relevance the accounts recounted above could have to Jaffna in the context of Ceylon's political history. They are very relevant for a number of reasons. In the first place, Tamils were seen as foreign invaders and Jaffna which became the eventual home for many invaders evidently posed a threat to the Sinhalese kingdoms in the south of the country. There was also the inherent threat of the Tamil culture which was considered vigorous with a well established permanent home in neighbouring India. Hence most Sinhalese con-

---

10. Morgan, W.S., *The Story of Malaya*, Malaya Publishing House, Singapore, 1949, pp 12-14.

sidered their culture fragile, requiring special safeguards if it was to co-exist with a more virile culture. For instance, an ardent advocate of Sinhalese nationalism raised some alarming questions when he wrote:—

> "For have not certain societies where traditional cultures were abandoned become extinct within our living memory? Some of the South Sea Islands have become depopulated. The Tasmanians are no more. The ancient cultures of Mayas and Incas have died out. The modern tribes of India are on the point of extinction. Why? ... No colonial people have contributed to human progress nor have they progressed themselves. All of them without exception were on the point of losing their soul and self-respect because of the suppression of traditional cultures and the imposition of alien cultures on unwilling minds ... what is native, what is tradition and what mattered were exchanged for the novel and the foreign."[11]

No doubt the writer had a particular audience in mind and succeeded in getting away with much too generalised and perhaps naïve arguments.

To cite another example, a select committee of the State Council was appointed in 1945 to examine the implications of replacing English by the gradual introduction of Sinhala and Tamil as the official languages. However, although the majority of the committee members thought that Tamil also should be given official status, they were clearly concerned about the future of the Sinhalese language on the grounds that it was solely confined to Ceylon, unlike Tamil which was "one of the best developed and most copious of Indian languages", not only used by nearly thirty million people in South India, but also recognised as an official language in other countries. The committee further pointed out that Sinhalese had not been recognised as a living language to serve as a medium for secondary or higher education until recent years and that it was not being used in business and commercial transactions, or in the courts of law and government. They therefore felt that the Sinhalese language needed to be saved and resuscitated by governmental action. In the event, the committee recommended a ten-year transition period, but the ministers led by D.S. Senanayake urged caution in proceeding speedily, and rather diplomatically avoided committing their party to any particular deadline for replacing English with the indigenous languages.[12]

---

11.   Wijesekara, N.D., Dynamism of Traditional Cultures, *Traditional Sinhalese Culture*, Peradeniya, ed., Pieris, R., 1956, pp 21-22.
12.   Sessional Paper xxii, Vol. 10, Ch's 1545-47, 1954, p11.

"It is popularly held," Howard Wriggins pointed out, "that since Tamil culture is so strong, it needs no state aid. There has therefore been a growing pressure to use the resources of the Ceylonese state for nurturing a purely Sinhalese art. Politicians have sought favour in their constituencies by urging the use of state funds to promote a cultural revival. The debates surrounding this budgetary issue have stirred community self-consciousness. Understandable Tamil reluctance to allow all cultural funds to go to Sinhalese cultural development has caused irritation among Sinhalese."[13]

Tamil impact on the politics of Ceylon was not necessarily by invasion and immigration or through the virility of Tamil culture. It was by invitation as well. It is interesting to note that Tamil connection was sought and established by Sinhalese royalty right from the beginning until the end of their rule with the fall of Kandy in 1815. It is claimed, for example, that Vijaya, the proclaimed precursor of the Sinhalese, sent messengers to the Pandyan kingdom in South India imploring the king to send him a bride. We are told that the king complied with the request and that the bride accompanied by a multitude of men and women of different ranks disembarked at 'Mahatittha', identified as Mantota in the northwest of Ceylon. It is also claimed that it was the advent of the South Indian bride that transformed the life of Vijaya, for the chronicler-historian Mahanama readily admits, "When he had forsaken his former evil ways, Vijaya, the Lord of men, ruling over all Lanka in peace and righteousness reigned, as is known in the city of Tambapanni for thirty eight years."[14]

Many historians believe that Tambapanni, which probably gave the name *Taprobane* to ancient Ceylon, was a derivation from the Tamraparni river just across Palk Strait on the South Indian coast. Nilakanta Sastri explains:

> "We may note that the Tamraparni, rising among the wooded hills of the southern ghats and benefiting from both the monsoons, forms a lifeline of agriculture in the Tinnevelly district. At its mouth, in the Gulf of Mannar are the famous Pearl fisheries ..."[15]

---

13. Wriggins, W.H., *Ceylon—Dilemmas of a New Nation*, op. cit., pp 241-42.
14. *Mahavamsa*, Ch.7, vv 72-74.
15. Nilakanta Sastri, K.A., *A History of South India*, Oxford University Press, 1958, p 44.

U.D. Jayasekara puts the whole picture in a more coherent context when he observes:—

> "It is possible that Tamil too may have been studied in early Ceylon, especially when we note that the Southern part of India has had connections with Ceylon from very ancient times. The Mahavamsa relates that Vijaya married a Pandya princess from Madhurai, and that she was accompanied by a hundred maidens and a thousand families of eighteen guilds who settled down in Ceylon. Coming to historical times, we find that two Tamils, Sena and Guttika, ruled at Anuradhapura in the latter half of the third century B.C. for a period of about twenty years. The famous Tamil king, Elara, reigned in Ceylon during the next century for a long period covering over forty years. By this time Tamil must have been well established in Ceylon. Large numbers of Tamil soldiers had already found their way to Ceylon, and Tamil merchants also had begun to engage in trade of different kinds ..."[16]

As for the political history of the Kandyan kingdom, M.R. Singer explains:—

> "It will be recalled that while the Sinhalese kings originally had come from South India, in the course of time they became culturally Sinhalese. In 1739, the last of these 'Sinhalese' kings, Rajasinha 1, died. Having no children of his own, the King before his death nominated as his successor the brother of his senior consort, an Indian from the Malabar coast. (S. D. Bailey, *Ceylon*, Hutchinson, 1952, p.63.) Had the Sinhalese aristocracy been able to agree among themselves, it is entirely possible that one of the many Sinhalese claimants for the throne might have been named. Since they could not agree, however, Rajasinha's Indian brother-in-law became king, thus establishing a new South Indian dynasty in Kandy."[17]

Sydney Bailey follows it up further by saying that the new king of Kandy "married a Malabar woman, and in 1751 his brother-in-law succeeded him as king, taking the title Kirti Sri. This man was not, of course, Sinhalese. His only claim to the throne of Kandy was that his Indian brother-in-law had been king before him, and his brother-in-law's only claim was that his three sisters had all been consorts of the last 'Sinhalese' king." This long line of Malabar rule by the *Nayakars,* as they were called, was very unpopular with the traditional Sinhalese chiefs

---

16.   Jayasekara, U.D., *Early History of Education in Ceylon*, op. cit., pp 163-64.
17.   Singer, M.R., *The Emerging Elite—A Study of Political Leadership in Ceylon*, MIT., Mass., 1964, p 29.

in particular and with the general public. As it turned out, it was left to a foreign power, this time the British, to do what the Sinhalese could not do themselves. The following extracts from the Kandyan Convention of 1815 illustrate this:

"... it is agreed and established as follows:

"That the Rajah Sri Wikreme Rajah Sinha by the habitual violation of the chief and most sacred duties of a Sovereign, has forfeited all claims to that title or the powers annexed to the same, and is declared fallen and deposed from the Office of King—His family and relatives ... for ever excluded from the throne—and all claim and title of the Malabar race to the dominion of the Kandyan Provinces is abolished and extinguished.

"That all male persons being or pretending to be relations of the late Rajah ... are hereby declared enemies to the Government of the Kandyan Provinces and excluded and prohibited from entering those Provinces on any pretext whatever, without a written permission of the British Government ...

The Dominion of the Kandyan Provinces is vested in the Sovereign of the British Empire ..."[18]

It must be noted that the word 'Malabar' was originally applied by the Portuguese not only to the people (and their language) on the west coast of South India, but also to the Tamil-speaking people throughout South India. As R. Caldwell explains: "The Portuguese ... sailing from Malabar on voyages of exploration ... made their acquaintance with various places on the eastern or Coromandel Coast ... and finding the language spoken by the fishing and sea-faring classes on the eastern coast similar to that spoken on the western, they came to the conclusion that it was identical with it, and called it in consequence by the same name, viz. Malabar."[19]

There is yet another aspect of politics in Ceylon that needs to be emphasised, and it is the involvement of the clergy in the political process of policy making. As Donald Smith has shown:

"While Buddhism is non-dogmatic and not based on any revelation of absolute truth, its adherents have nevertheless been extremely conscious of the uniqueness of their message. Buddhism has been a missionary religion ever

---

18.   Baily, S.D., *CEYLON*, op.cit., pp.83-84.
19.   Caldwell, R., *A Comparative Grammar of the Dravidian or South Indian Family of Languages*, 2nd ed., Madras, 1875, pp.10-12.

since the Buddha sent out his followers to spread the *Dhamma*, a universal teaching which would bring enlightenment to all men. Buddhism differs significantly from Hinduism in this conviction that there is after all one known path to perfect enlightenment, and that the Buddha has discovered it. Within the Buddhist monastic order there has been a strong emphasis on the preservation of doctrinal purity, and rulers have from time to time intervened in order to suppress heretical elements in the *Sangha*, sometimes resorting to violent means. Buddhism is not as tolerant as Hinduism with the latter's constant emphasis on many ways, many paths."[20]

On the question of Buddhist ecclesiastical organisation, having said that the Buddha had "promulgated detailed rules governing life in the *Sangha*," Smith goes on to observe that the *Sangha* "not only commands the reverence of the laity but is organised in such a way that it can effectively mobilize public opinion. If the leadership should desire a political role for the *Sangha*, there is no doubt about its ability to fulfil it, despite the *Vinaya* rules of monastic discipline which forbid a monk's involvement in mundane political affairs. The political potential of the *Sangha* in Ceylon and Burma has already been impressively demonstrated. The *Sangha* can readily become a vigorous pressure group demanding for Buddhism the place traditionally accorded it by the state. Organizations of Buddhist laymen can also play an important role. The All-Ceylon Buddhist Congress, for example, with the support of prominent leaders of the *Sangha*, has had considerable influence in promoting the role of Buddhism in national life and in urging the government to do the same."[21]

It cannot come as a surprise, therefore, that the Oxford educated and one time popular politician, Solomon West Ridgeway Dias Bandaranaike, the Prime Minister of Ceylon, was assassinated by a Buddhist monk in 1959, although he had already pandered to the wishes of the Buddhist clergy by making Sinhala the Official Language in 1956, as he was viewed as a traitor to the Buddhist cause in the long run. Yet the manner in which the assassination was reported by the government and the media, deliberately to muddle the situation and rouse communal tensions, is still vivid in the memories of those citizens who had hoped that at long last there was some hope of reconciliation and national regeneration.

---

20. Smith, D.E., *The Political Implications of Asian Religions*, Princeton, N.J., 1966, pp 12-15.
21. Ibid.

The entire nation was appalled to hear the news of the assassination on the radio, repeated every few minutes, that the Prime Minister had been shot by an assassin 'dressed as a Buddhist monk', followed by the exhortation that the public should remain calm! It was the most diabolical act of depravity and, for all intents and purposes, the future of the country was put on hold. All citizens, whatever their race or religion or language, saw the danger signals orchestrated from the highest echelons of power, portending a paralysis to afflict the nation for years. Politics has not been the same since.

One is reminded of a Taoist verse, which runs:

> A centipede was happy quite
> Until a toad in fun
> Asked it which leg came after which?
> This wrought it up to such a pitch
> It fell exhausted in a ditch
> Not knowing how to run!

6

EDUCATIONAL

It was seen in Chapter 3 that the intellectual tradition in Jaffna had led to a significant output of literary works from early times. S. Arasaratnam says:—

> "From an early date education spread among the people, creating a literate community which remains so to this day. Temple schools and improvised classes on the outer verandah of the village schoolmaster's house spread basic education to the rural areas. Toward the end of the fifteenth century an academy of Tamil literature was founded in Nallur by the king. The academy did useful work in collecting and preserving ancient classical Tamil works in manuscript form. Some historical literature was attempted during this period and some translations and adaptations from Sanskrit works."[1]

Where the goal of life was conceived as the individual's need for self-realisation, life itself was inevitably seen as an educational process, and education as a life-long process. In the *Guru-Sishya* tradition which Jaffna had imbibed from its culturally powerful neighbour South India, the family of the guru provided not only the physical embodiment of a classroom to the pupil, but a wholesome natural environment for an integrated development of the pupil's personality. With the crude metal stylus and segments of the Palmyra leaf serving as the only aids for writing, the oral tradition of teaching and learning in an improvised classroom, either in the teachers' home or in the temple-hall nearby, often under a moonlit sky, obviously had to overcome many impediments.

Intellect has been characterised by Jacques Barzun as a social phenomenon, as well as an aspect of culture, which he goes on to describe as community property. It means that it can be handed down from one generation to another. He calls it the 'House of Intellect', because, he argues, "it is an establishment, requiring

---

1.   Arasaratnam, S., *CEYLON*, Prentice Hall, N.J., 1964, p 115.

appurtenances and prescribing conventions." In fact, Barzun goes further to explain:—

> "From the image of a house and its economy, one can see what an inquiry into the institution of Intellect must include. The main topics are: the state of the language, the system of schooling, the means and objects of communication, the supplies of money for thought and learning, and the code of feeling and conduct that goes with them. When the general tendency of these arrangements makes for order, logic, clarity, and speed of communication, one may say that a tradition of Intellect exists."[2]

A note of caution, though, comes from Anthony Wallace:—

> "But we should not confine our discussion of intellect to the last few centuries of western Europe and the Americas. There was, for instance, a scholastic intellect which developed in the medieval religious tradition. There was a tradition of the intellect among the followers of Mohammed; and, likewise, among Indian, Chinese, and other civilized peoples. It would be possible, indeed, to argue that intellect has its own tradition and its own problems, in most if not all cultures, even though its house may be small and contain only a few specialists in law, religion, politics, warfare, irrigation technology, astrology, or what have you. For the utility of intellect springs from the fact that it is the only truly universal tool, capable of maintaining and restoring human arrangements against the erosions of time, capable of recognising and solving new problems as well as learning the answers to old ones …"[3]

Education, standing as it does on the bedrock of philosophical idealism, including religious scholasticism, came to be deeply ingrained in the psyche of the Jaffna Tamils through centuries of contact with South India and the wider world it opened up. Thus Education with a capital E constituted the central plank of the social edifice, to the extent that a vast body of literature spanning a wide horizon, both in time and space, became readily available for both the adult as well as the newly initiated child to immerse freely. Education in its broad sense thus symbolised the purpose of life itself, the very essence of one's existence—indeed, the pinnacle of one's possession. Education has, in fact, been emphasised in many

2. Barzun, J., *The House of Intellect*, Secker and Warburg, London, 1961, pp 4-6.
3. Wallace, A.F.C., Schools in Revolutionary and Conservative Societies, *Cultural Relevance and Educational Issues—Readings in Anthropology and Education*, Eds., Ianni, F.A.J., and Storey, E., Little, Brown & Co., Canada, 1973, pp 235-38.

literary compositions as the most beautiful and valuable possession anyone could aspire for.

The educational experience of the average Tamil child involved listening to a series of folk tales, songs and verses etc. inculcating religious, moral and social obligations, and participating in ceremonies, including those associated with initiation into learning and adulthood. As the child grew older, values were reinforced by contact with cultural agents mainly through institutions like the caste system and the extended family. Writing on 'Culture and Personality', George Spindler observed:—

> "We know that human beings achieve human status by learning, and this learning must take place in a social environment that is never wholly unique and is always structured in some degree by whatever cultural norms govern the behaviour of the people in their society." In other words, "at a certain stage in the child's development most of the latent learning he has acquired about the values and ethics of his group up to that time is made highly explicit and given a great deal of verbal reinforcement, and thereby, personality structure is created through educational experience."[4]

Among the immense body of Tamil literary works that were available to the learner were the *Edduthokai* (The Eight Anthologies), considered unique and powerful, and rich in vivid realism, the epic *Chilappathikaram* (The Ankle Bracelet), which through its moving story of true human love and baroque splendour of lyrical poetry has earned a place among the masterpieces of the world, and the *Thirukkural* (Ethical Maxims) in distich form, which was eulogised by Albert Schweitzer as follows: "There hardly exists in the literature of the world a collection of maxims in which we find so much lofty wisdom."[5]

The two great epic poems of India, the *Mahabarata* and the *Ramayana*, compared by many authorities with the twin epics of Greek literature, the *Iliad* and the *Odyssey* respectively, which were made widely available to Tamil audiences through scholarly translations, have been very popular in Jaffna, too, over the centuries. As Milton Singer observes in relation to South India, "perhaps the most striking aspect of the continuity in culture between village and city is the common stock of mythological and legendary themes shared by both villager and

---

4.   Spindler, G. D., Ed., *Education and Culture—Anthropological Approaches*, Holt, Rinehart and Winston, Inc., 1963, pp 35 and 352-382.

5.   Schweitzer, A., *Indian Thought and Its Development*, op. cit., p 203.

the city man. The same stories from the *Ramayana,* the *Bhagavatapurana,* and the *Mahabharata* are recited, sung, and played in both village and city."[6] The observations of Milton Singer are as applicable to the Tamil parts of Ceylon, and Jaffna in particular, where certain families are known by the characters their forbears played in the enactment of dramatised episodes from these epics in the past, and to this day, there are also place names that owe their origin to these captivating dramatic themes.

The point that needs to be underscored is that while informal education that evolved over many centuries helped to reinforce codes of conduct, standards of behaviour, acts of valour, chivalry and compassion etc., in addition to promoting literacy among the populace, formal education which was necessarily confined to the privileged few, had the effect of refining and expanding the educational material available to the community at large.

The advent of western powers obviously had a very major impact on the kind of education provided, the methods used to impart knowledge, as well as the whole area of educational provision. It was the policy of the Portuguese and the Dutch to use the indigenous languages as the media of instruction. When it came to the establishment of schools in the areas that came under their influence, the colonial powers found in Jaffna a more fertile and favourable ground for intensive educational provision than in any other part of the country. Of the Portuguese period, for instance, W.R. Muelder had observed:

> "The situation in Jaffnapatam, which became a Portuguese province in 1621, was more favourable to intensive educational and missionary work than was Colombo, for it was isolated from the reactionary influence of interior Ceylon and also by the sea; its children earned the reputation of being the best educated in the Far East."[7]

On the other hand, there was evidently a suppression of the traditional system of education in Jaffna. "Whatever educational institutions existed among the Hindus in the North undoubtedly suffered under Portuguese rule. King Sankili of Jaffna was captured by the Portuguese in 1621, and with his capture the Hindu system of education went underground, a little teaching being secretly imparted in some houses or *Thinnai* (outer verandah or foyer) by ardent Hindus who were

6.   Singer, M., *WHEN A GREAT TRADITION MODERNIZES*, op. cit., pp 74-75.
7.   Muelder, W.R., *Schools For A New Nation*, K.V.G. De Silva and Sons, Colombo, 1962, p 15.

determined not to let the torch of learning entirely die out. In so far as the Dutch period is concerned, while there is little doubt that there was the same kind of suppression of Hindu education by the Dutch as by the Portuguese, it has been claimed that there was ... a good output of Hindu literature during this period."[8] However, as Muelder pointed out:

> "... it would be exceedingly wrong to undervalue the educational system of the Dutch. When it was at its best in the eighteenth century, the school attendance averaged about 70,000, a figure which was not reached for another three-quarters of a century ... The impact of the Dutch on Ceylon, especially in education, ushered in the modern period for the culture of the Island. It is to the Dutch that is owed the beginnings of this modern era though the changes they introduced affected the people of the country only to a small extent. But it was in education that the most telling blows were to strike for even in England during the eighteenth century, elementary education was not so widespread as in the Dutch territory in Ceylon."[9]

There is no doubt that Jaffna was in the lead again, although it must be admitted that most of the education imparted was closely linked to religious instruction. Too much time appears to have been devoted to eradicating Popish teachings and instituting Calvinistic tenets. Philippus Baldaeus, for example, cited the school at Pandeterippu in Jaffna as exemplary for the reason that its 600 pupils had made such progress that they could "refute the Popish errors concerning purgatory, the Mass, indulgencies and auricular confession."[10]

During the British rule, it was in Jaffna that the Missionaries concentrated on providing for English education, and as a direct consequence the policy of government aid to mission schools was initiated. Ludowyk explains that "typical of life in Jaffna was the smallholder, aided by his family in working the land, strongly conservative, but well aware of the advantage of education. It was in the north that the system of mission schools receiving grants for their educational

---

8.   Jayasuriya, J.E., *Educational Policies And Progress During British Rule In Ceylon (Sri Lanka)* 1796-1948, Associated Educational Publishers, Ceylon, 1976, p 20.

9.   Muelder, W.R., *Schools For A New Nation*, op. cit., pp 25-26.

10.   Baldaeus, P., Description of Coromandel and Ceylon, *A Collection of Voyages and Travels, 1744-46*, ed. Churchill, A&J, Churchill, London, Vol.3, p 714.

work from the government first developed."[11] As K.M. De Silva, too, has pointed out:—

"It was in Jaffna ... where the Missionaries laid great emphasis on English education, that the system of aid to mission schools really took root. The first School Commission had started an English school and four vernacular schools there, but these proved to be unsatisfactory and were closed down in 1842. In 1843 other schools were opened under new teachers, but they never really started, as the School Commission found it difficult to superintend these schools effectively. Besides, the mission schools were so well established that the Government saw no need to compete with them. The Government schools were closed and, instead, grants were made to missions ... with the stipulation that this money was to be spent *in addition* to the amounts already devoted by these missions to the diffusion of English education."[12]

De Silva went on to claim that "since 1843, the Government had left the three missions—the C.M.S., the Wesleyans and the American Mission—in charge of education, and merely provided them with an annual grant of money. This system had proved to be so successful that there was no necessity for purely Government Schools."[13]

With increasing demand for English education, religious and political leaders, as well as educators and the general public, began to take an active interest in educational provision and policy. Realising the need for a comprehensive policy on education, a motion was introduced in the Legislative Council by the Tamil member, Muthu Coomaraswamy, proposing the appointment of a Committee to look into it, and on the proposal being accepted, the Morgan Committee on Education was appointed in 1865. The Report of the Committee, of which Muthu Coomaraswamy was a member, which was accepted by the Government in 1868, became the first coherent, albeit controversial, policy on education since the Colebrooke Report of 1832. The main recommendations of the Report were the creation of a State Education Department, strengthening of the popular denominational system, a dual language policy, and a more balanced curriculum to meet the needs of the colonial economy.

---

11. Ludowyk, E.F.C., *The Story of Ceylon*, op. cit., p 223.
12. De Silva, K.M., *Social Policy and Missionary Organization in Ceylon* 1840-1855, op. cit., pp 157 & 174.
13. Ibid.

Following the Morgan Committee's recommendations, the Department of Public Instruction was established in 1870, followed by a gradual increase in the number of both English and vernacular schools. Needless to say, the Jaffna public seized the opportunity with open arms, and they have never regretted it. There was a significant increase in the number of grant-aided denominational schools, mostly in Jaffna because of greater public support and demand. For as Howard Wriggins noted:

> "It was the peoples from the north—the Tamils—who first experienced the pressures of overpopulation and limited local resources. Hence, the growing public service presented itself as a career for which they were well suited by virtue of another historical circumstance. More missionary schools in relation to the population had been established in Tamil areas than in Sinhalese areas. Tamil children were good at figures and their parents goaded them in their academic work for fear of unemployment or hard labour as the price of failure. In addition, their religious beliefs allowed them wide latitude in adopting foreign ways for work purposes without disturbing their fundamental Hindu traditions. Their schools prepared them for government service and teaching posts, and they found jobs in many parts of the island."[14]

The American Board of Missions confined themselves to Jaffna and its environs, and the Baptist Mission was the only one not to establish schools in the north or the east of the country. The two most influential Missions, the Church Missionary Society and the Methodists, went so far as to observe two separate administrative divisions for the Northern and Southern regions of Ceylon.

Island-wide, the number of grant-aided schools increased from 229 in 1870 to 1328 in 1900, of which a large proportion were obviously in Jaffna, in consideration of the fact that apart from the general trend for the Christian missionaries to be more attracted to Jaffna, some denominations were particularly concentrated in Jaffna, as, for instance, the Hindu Board of Education which managed 45 schools in 1900 as against none in 1870, and the American Mission schools that increased from 44 in 1870 to 129 in 1900.

The work of the American Mission in Jaffna deserves special mention, in view of its pioneering and egalitarian nature. In the first place, the Mission established Village or Native schools, providing instruction in Tamil and arithmetic, and also Religious Studies. They also established three Central Day Schools for able stu-

---

14.   Wriggins, W.H., *Ceylon—Dilemmas of a New Nation*, op. cit., p 234.

dents selected from the Village or Native schools. The curriculum in the Central Day Schools was much wider and included English as a subject. The Mission then proceeded to establish two Charity Boarding Schools, one for boys and the second for girls. Importantly, students of ability selected by independent assessment from the elementary schools were given free education at these Charity Boarding Schools, which included all expenses covering their board and lodging. The curriculum was the same as in the Central Day Schools, but the innovative idea of providing education in a residential environment for the able but depressed and underprivileged children, especially in a caste-ridden society, did create tremendous problems for the management. But it is to their credit that they managed to weather the storm, and eventually succeeded in creating an uneasy conscience among the complacent conservative majority. On the educational front, the American Mission was commended by the Colebrooke Commission for their outstanding contribution to education, especially for the teaching of English and the Humanities. To crown their achievements, the American Mission also established in 1827 an institution called the Batticotta Seminary for further and higher education, which has grown to maturity as the leading educational institution in Jaffna, appropriately called Jaffna College.

Other missionary bodies followed suit and in the course of the next few years many schools were established in Jaffna. As a matter of fact, the increase in the number of state aided denominational schools far exceeded the rate at which state schools were established, notably in Jaffna, for reasons already mentioned. On a national scale for which statistics are available, grant-aided schools increased from 229 in 1870 to 1328 in 1900, as against 156 to 500 state schools for the same period. It may be noted, however, that even as early as 1856, 33 of the 36 state schools in the Northern Province were managed for the Government by the three missions—American (17), Methodist (10) and Church Missionary Society (6), and the *Government Almanac* for that year published a total figure of 89 state schools in the country, which included just three state schools in the North!

For a time, of course, only middle class jobs were available to the English educated, but soon with the expansion of educational provision and more specialised education being provided by schools, recognised professions like medicine, engineering, accounting and law etc were within their reach.

There is no doubt that in the competition for jobs in the government and the private sector as well as in the leading professions, the Jaffna Tamils did have an edge over the rest of the country by virtue of the educational provision in the district. So that when the University College and later the University of Ceylon were set up in Ceylon, the Jaffna Tamils were naturally not slow to take the initial advantage, with the schools rising to the occasion to cater to the ever increasing demand for access to university education. Of course, the students or their parents or even the schools could not be taken to task for opting for the best opportunities available in a competitive market. But then, there came the proverbial *Sword of Damocles* to hang over the heads of aspiring young Tamils, when the Commission on Higher Education produced a majority report recommending that in the interests of equality of opportunity, provision had to be made to admit *at least* 6 Sinhalese speaking students as against one Tamil speaking student to places in higher education. This gross act of betrayal of the Tamil speaking youth of the country is still alive in the hearts and minds of those generations who have had to live with it, but a great many sought opportunities elsewhere.

There have been some glaring drawbacks no doubt in the kind of education provided in schools. To some extent the wishes of people like Robert Fellowes seem to have materialised with devastating consequences, for it was he who urged almost two centuries ago, "Let her (Britain) sedulously labour to diffuse her vernacular idiom through all her foreign settlements and let her regard it as the best means of facilitating the greatest of all human works—the intellectual improvement of Man."[15] Fellowes would have been delighted to walk down the streets of twenty first century Jaffna studded with children's nurseries catering to his elitist ego, for he would have heard the children sing the very same rhymes sung by British children umpteen years ago. However, fifty years after him the Morgan Committee on Education (1865) did observe that what the education system had succeeded in producing was "a class of shallow, conceited, half-educated youths who have learned nothing but to look back with contempt upon the conditions in which they were born and from which they conceive that their education has raised them, and who desert the ranks of the industrious classes to become idle, discontented hangers on of the Courts and Public Offices." In fact, the Committee was merely quoting one of the Inspectors of Schools, who had been rather harsh in his criticism, but as Dr. P. Udagama, Director-General of Education, pointed out a century later: "Our school curriculum however has not changed in a significant way over a century ... A distaste for work has been created in the child. The child no longer cherishes the work of his parents or the social values of the home. Our education system is not related to the social environment in which it is situated ..."[16]

---

15. Fellowes, R., *History of Ceylon*, London, 1817, p 228.

The stark reality was that the expansion of the school system that controlled learning, was confined to imparting formal instruction in specific subjects, to the exclusion of the kind of comprehensive learning required for people to contribute to the wider needs of society. On the other hand, whatever provision for learning that was available in the wider sectors of the economy became increasingly inadequate in the context of the rapid economic and social changes that were taking place. What was sadly lacking was the provision to educate the workforce that was needed for national development.

The problem was clearly seen by the National Education Commission under the Chairmanship of Professor J.E. Jayasuriya of the University of Ceylon, whose Report was published in 1962. The Commission referred to legislation in a number of countries to relate education to the needs of the community and went on to make specific recommendations to include some basic quota of 'work experience' in the school curriculum. The White Paper on Education that followed too contained definite proposals to make the curriculum more balanced to reflect the needs of the community. However, a pilot National Service Scheme that was launched by the Department of Education covering all schools and training colleges became a dead letter within a matter of two to three years.

A comprehensive survey carried out by the present writer in Jaffna at the time revealed some of the reasons why the National Service Scheme failed as it did. The most important reason was the apathy shown by the Principals of schools generally, although there were some exceptions. The second reason was that students on the whole were made to take part in the kind of work or services in which they were not at all interested, although 99 per cent of the student population said that they welcomed the proposed changes in the curriculum. One student observed: "… any attempt to improve the village is an attempt to improve the economy of Ceylon"—while another said, "I like to take part in any project that would serve humanity"; and yet a third student observed rather philosophically: "I like to serve in a place that is backward in finance as well as in human culture!"

Certain genuine difficulties were also brought to light by the survey. Difficulties of finance and organisation, lack of cooperation by parents, and barriers of class and caste prejudice were highlighted as the main obstacles to be overcome. The

16.   Udagama, P., Text of a Talk at a Symposium organised by the National Education Society of Ceylon, 16 October, 1971.

success of any proposed changes to the school curriculum would no doubt depend on the extent to which those in charge of institutions like schools and colleges, including government departments, are prepared to learn from experience.

Yet a few successful inroads in community development were seen in Jaffna, and one of them deserves to be mentioned. The train from Colombo that steamed into the Jaffna Railway Station at 6 a.m. on 19 April 1964 carried an unusual cargo—volunteers from the South of the country who had gone to take part in a six-day work camp to link two villages, Neervely and Kaithady, by a one and a half mile-long roadway. The work camp had been sponsored by the All-Ceylon Gandhi Seva Sangham and the Sarvodaya Shramadana Movement of Ceylon. Two hundred and eight students and adults representing twenty-seven schools in the South participated, while two hundred and thirty five students and adults represented thirteen schools and other institutions in Jaffna.

In the early hours of the morning of 20 April, the villagers of Neervely, disturbed from their traditional slumber, looked on as the procession of volunteers wended its way to the work site, about a mile from the camp. The large number of onlookers cheered as the first few sods were cut, and the six-day project was on.

Working hours in the morning were from 6 to 10 and in the evening from 3.30 to 7. Time was set apart for relaxation, group discussions and educational and cultural activities. As it was the first work camp of its kind and scope to be attempted in Jaffna, an evaluation of its significance would be worthwhile. In the first place, it was indeed significant that two rather conservative villages were willing to partner in a joint project beneficial to both, an event unique in the history of local community participation. Secondly, not only did the two Village Committees, Rural Development Societies and some voluntary organisations make available the essential equipment needed for a project of such a magnitude, they also undertook to host the participating volunteers. The third noteworthy feature was that a general committee of the work camp and a number of sub-committees consisting of local men and women worked out the detailed day-to-day arrangements. It was especially significant too that the project involved two typical villages where students from the town had the opportunity to learn something of village life and the inter-dependence of town and village, for as Vinoba Bhave had observed from the vantage point of his wide experience in India, "Every village, no matter how small, is a microcosm; it contains the whole world in miniature, and a complete education must be obtainable there." And lastly, the work camp was also aimed at inculcating a sense of the dignity of labour.

When one looks at the tangible results of the project, the major achievement was that it provided a road that shortened the normal travelling distance between the two villages by five miles. In so doing it also connected two crucial market centres in the two villages, Chunnakam and Chavakachcheri, by a shorter route, making them more accessible to buyers and sellers, and a veritable boon to farmers, particularly in the deep rural countryside. Where there was a road open for villagers to market their produce, there was also a road open to prosperity, to progress!

The second achievement, perhaps less tangible, but of great potential, was that if two groups of people belonging to two different communities, speaking two different languages and professing many faiths, could live as one family within the confines of a work camp, and work in unison with a common objective in mind, it was indeed a lesson for the whole nation. *The Sunday Times* that published the above evaluation by the present writer gave it the appropriate heading—*A ROAD CALLED UNITY, ONE AND A HALF MILES LONG!*

> *Upon this darling of Ceylon*
> *May Seva, mighty name!*
> *Protector of this mundane egg*
> *Bestow eternal fame!*
>
> T.A. Anderson[17]

---

17.   Anderson, T.A., *Poems Written Chiefly in India*, London, 1809, p.63.

7

CO-OPERATIVE INITIATIVES

"From India and the Golden Chersonese,
And utmost Indian isle Taprobane,
Dusk faces with white silken turbants wreathed;"

So wrote John Milton in *Paradise Regained* (Book 4), 1671.

Chersonese comes from the Latin *Chersonesus* for peninsula. It is a reference to an ancient region corresponding to the Thracian or Gallipoli Peninsula north of Hellespont, which serves to link the Aegean Sea to the Sea of Marmora, providing a route between Europe and Asia. The name is also sparingly used to describe other peninsulas. In the lines above, the reference is clearly to the northern extremity of the Jaffna Peninsula jutting into the Indian Ocean, opening a shielded sea route between East and West through the Palk Strait and the Gulf of Mannar.

As for *Taprobane*, reference has been made already in Chapter 5 to the Tamraparni River in South India emptying into the Gulf of Mannar, famous for its Pearl fisheries, which probably gave the Greek name *Taprobane* to ancient Ceylon. "This is the great island in the ocean, lying in the Indian Sea. By the Indians it is called *Sielediba*, but by the Greeks *Taprobane*."[1] There was evidently great demand for the pearls of *Chilapathurai*, the name by which the Mannar coast was known, and the pearls found there, which were considered pristine, were given the special name *Tamaravarnika* after the name of the famous river.

---

1.   *Cosmas*, Bk. xi.

Many a seafarer and writer had commented on the strategic and busy thorough-fare the Northern Gulf provided not only between East and West, but also between South India and North Ceylon historically.

As Ludowyk observes:

> "As an island on the highways of trade of West with East, even in those ear-lier days when West was India and East China, Ceylon was continually attracting various peoples to its shores. Besides the constant stream from India there were traders and seafarers from Arabia, Africa, from the islands of the Malayan Archipelago, and from China ...

> Moreover as tropical island, well-watered, with its lush vegetation and cli-mate tempered by the sea, Ceylon has been a powerful magnet. Its precious stones, their value fabulously exaggerated, were the subject of legends to be found in *The Arabian Nights.* At times the attraction of the island seemed to lie not in the resources which differentiated it from the continent of India, but in its similarities with it. South India in ancient times—the Dravidian country—was flourishing and prosperous. It throve on the trade which took the luxuries of India, China and the East to the Graeco-Roman world. Yet wave after wave of invaders from the continent broke upon the island. Cey-lon drew them as it was a country like their own, into which South Indian people were continually pressing."[2]

Even the *Mahavamsa* records that eighteen guilds of merchants accompanied the Pandyan princess who came to Ceylon on the invitation of Vijaya to become his queen. Many inscriptions in South India give accounts of institutions like guilds and corporate bodies that functioned to provide common services. For instance, *Kuri* and *Perunkuri*, later known as *Ur* were in charge of village administration. The working committees were known as *Kanam* and their executive committees named *Variam*.

Nagaram was yet another body consisting mainly of merchants or traders cum occupational groups. *Manigramam* and *Anjuvanam* are also corporate bodies mentioned among the more influential ones, but the most celebrated was called *Nanadesi Tissaiyayirathu Ainnuttuvar,* whose five hundred members went to dif-ferent countries in a thousand directions, as the name suggests.

---

2.   Ludowyk, E.F.C., *The Story of Ceylon*, op. cit., p 23.

One of the cave inscriptions of Ceylon belonging to the Second century B.C. refers to "a corporation of Tamil merchants, of which the captain of a ship (*Navika*) was the head."[3]

The western areas of the *Wanni*, where Mantota, the ancient port of Ceylon was situated, in or near Mannar, must have been a hive of activity as many abandoned tanks and channels bear testimony. *Kurichakulam Tekam* on the *Kal Aru* is one of the many dams abandoned. Some stone pillars mark what was once probably an ancient shrine at *Komputukki* between *Vidataltivu* and *Iluppaikadavai*. There are remnants of ancient routes that connected *Mantota* with Anuradhapura and Jaffna, as well as ruins of ancient bridges. All available evidence suggests that there was a lot of commercial and socio-economic activity going on in the region until some destructive forces, natural or human, intervened.

According to historical sources, Anuradhapura was the capital city for long periods until foreign invasions forced the capital to be moved. Rhoads Murphey observes that "Anuradhapura was the capital and primate city until 1017, when following a destructive invasion by the Cholas from South India, the capital was moved to Polonnaruwa.... Anuradhapura's port was the ancient city of Mantota, through which it conducted overseas trade (largely in foreign hands), and in particular maintained its close relations with South India, although these were often in the undesirable form of invasions. It was in fact the repeated invasions, to which Anuradhapura was dangerously exposed, which must have dictated the shift of the capital to Polonnaruwa in 1017 following the Chola sack of Anuradhapura ...

> "The Chola conquest of 1017 was part of their expansion under Rajendra 1 from their base in South India as far as Malaya and Indonesia. Theirs was only the most successful of a long series of invasions, most of them of the nature of raiding parties, which plagued Raja Rata periodically from the time of Vijaya's legendary landing in the sixth century B.C. No succeeding century was free from them, and on repeated occasions they drove the Sinhalese power into the hills for short periods. Often they were accompanied or followed by internal dissension when rival Sinhalese claimants to the throne made common cause with the raiders or invaders or took advantage of the

---

3.   Inscription No.12 from Periya-Puliyankulam, *Journal of the Royal Asiatic Society*, Ceylon Branch, No.93, pp 54-55.

king's weakness for their own ends. Nearly half of the time until the thirteenth century was occupied by invasions or raids, or by civil war."[4]

What comes out clearly is that in spite of some traditions of corporate or co-operative activities in certain relatively peaceful times, the atmosphere in Ceylon, on the whole, was not conducive to co-operative effort. Was it true of Jaffna too?

Apart from invasions, intrigue and internal dissension, there was in fact one other reason for the decline of the Dry Zone in general. Here's Rhoads Murphey again:

"Dry-zone rainfall is derived primarily from the northeast monsoon, which blows over Ceylon from late October into January. About 80 per cent of the annual dry-zone rainfall occurs in the hundred days between October and January, but even this period may witness disastrous dry spells. Soils are highly porous and shallow, and impervious bedrock is only one to fifty feet from the surface, so that groundwater resources are slight and cannot be depended on, with few local variations, for the support of agriculture. The Jaffna peninsula in the north, underlain by limestone strata, is an exception and supports an intensive agriculture mainly from wells, aside from the largely rain-fed rice."[5]

Long periods of drought, soil exhaustion and relative infertility of the soil under expansive cultivation in the Dry Zone were no doubt factors that gave Jaffna a comparative edge over the rest of the Dry Zone. Then, of course, there is no substitute for industry and perseverance.

In much the same way as William Colebrooke and Charles Cameron were driven by a Benthamite mission in making their recommendations for legislative and judicial reforms respectively in 1832, which were far in advance of the time, and eventually foundered in hazardous political waters, many a reform overdue awaited the emergence of enlightened leadership, which, in the absence of local initiative, had to come from a rare breed of colonial administrators.

Notable among those civil servants who led the way was Sir James Emerson-Tennent, Colonial Secretary of the Government of Ceylon from 1845 to 1850. An intellectual with a Benthamite zeal, his two major works *Christianity in Ceylon*

---

4.   Murphey, R., The Ruin of Ancient Ceylon, *Journal of Asian Studies*, op.cit., pp 185 et seq.
5.   Ibid., p 182.

(London, 1850) and *Ceylon* (Two Volumes, London, 1857) were serious studies with a great deal of insight, that had far-reaching implications for colonial policy for a long time. No less perceptive were his Despatches to the Colonial Office on a variety of subjects, sometimes covering difficult and sensitive areas such as Commerce, Finance, Immigrant Indian Labour and the problems associated with it, and Religious implications.

A succession of civil servants, some with an Owenite vision, whose apprenticeship had been shaped on the anvil of colonial administration, especially in India, were mainly responsible for ushering in the Co-operative Movement in Ceylon in the early part of the twentieth century, as well as tending the delicate plant during its early and formative years.

Dobbs from a scholarly point of view contends that the 'Rochdale Pioneers' of 1844 recognised Robert Owen as their prophet and "laboured in a soil already prepared." He goes on to substantiate his thesis by asserting that the early co-operators and their successors at Rochdale "belonged to that class among the poor to whom Wesley had appealed with greatest effect," and that both John Wesley and Owen believed in "the universality of their mission." He crowns his argument by stating that whereas "one claimed the world for his parish, the other founded an association which was to embrace mankind."[6]

Both Cole and Postgate support Dobbs by pointing out that the members of the 'Redemptionist' movement, established in Leeds in 1846 on Owenite foundations, played a leading role in establishing the Leeds Co-operative Society, which was to become "one of the most successful in the country". They "worked in with the Christian Socialists in the Co-operative Ventures of the early 'fifties", and "Parliament, so suspicious towards Trade Unions, looked indulgently upon the Co-operatives, largely because of Christian Socialist influence ..."[7]

It is the generally accepted view of students of peoples' movements that the so called Co-operative Crusade was in many respects a secular version of the Methodist message, a missionary zeal brought to bear on bread and butter issues.

---

6.   Dobbs, A.E., *Education and Social Movements* 1700-1850, Longmans, Green, 1919, pp 213-27.
7.   Cole, G.D.H. & Postgate, R., *The Common People* 1746-1946, Methuen, London, 1963, pp 318-19; 380-81.

The foregoing synopsis of early co-operative initiatives in Britain serves to emphasise the immensity of problems that confronted both the initiators of co-operative action in Ceylon, as well as those whose responsibility it was to implement the proposals at various levels.

Paradoxically though the co-operative system that was introduced to Ceylon by the British Government was not one based on the 'Rochdale' or British model. It was, indeed, of an alien parentage.

In the history of the Co-operative Movement in Ceylon, the rapid expansion of the plantation economy and the accompanying decline of subsistence agriculture played a crucial part. For one thing, the capital-intensive plantation sector could not sit comfortably with the traditional subsistence economy based largely on customary laws and practices, including property rights.

The new land laws introduced by the British had far reaching consequences. During the early days of British rule no European was allowed to hold land for more than seven years, except in Colombo, the capital city. With the opening up of plantations by the beginning of the nineteenth century the restriction on land ownership by foreign citizens was removed, and a Government Proclamation in 1812 made it legal for Europeans and others to receive grants of land, not exceeding 1000 acres, free of tax for five years. Land grants were made to civil and military officials, too, to experiment in coffee plantation. With the opening up of tea and rubber plantations, there was an unprecedented demand for estate holdings from all who had the clout, including some Governors, top civil servants and military officials.

By Ordinance 12 of 1840 all forests, wasteland sites, unoccupied and uncultivated lands were declared Crown Land, which also applied to *Chena* plots, that is, land cleared for cultivation by the burning of forests, which was a customary practice. In short, large chunks of land were given away regardless of the consequences on traditional methods of cultivation of rice and other subsidiary food crops.

The last straw to break the camel's back, as it were, was the Grain Tax on rice cultivation. Criticising the tax in 1845 Sir James Emerson-Tennent had remarked that "… it would be difficult to devise a scheme more pregnant with oppression, extortion and demoralisation."[8]

On the Governor's recommendation, the Secretary of State appointed a Commission of Inquiry, which reported in 1849. In recommending a general land tax the Commission observed that it had no doubt whatsoever as to "the oppression and extortion committed under the system of farming out the annual assessment on paddy lands, the discouragement which it causes to the cultivation of that description of produce, and the demoralisation which tyranny and avarice on the one side, and cunning and deception on the other, necessarily create among all who are connected with it."[9] As a result of continued criticism of the Grain Tax and persistent agitation from various interests, the tax was finally abolished in 1892.

The abolition of the Grain Tax had the unprecedented effect of mobilising public opinion to seek redress in whichever quarter it was deemed necessary. The legal system on the whole was unfavourable to the smallholder. It soon became evident that it was not borrowing as such that affected productivity in agriculture, but indebtedness, and that if there were reasonable arrangements in place for a loan to be repaid within a stipulated period, then notwithstanding the size of the loan it was sound use of credit, and there could be no question of indebtedness or insolvency. On the contrary, if the farmer was unable to settle his debt without disposing of his assets or declaring bankruptcy, or where he had to pledge his labour and that of his family, as was the practice in many areas, including Jaffna, then there was a state of irredeemable indebtedness and subservience affecting productivity. If organised credit could be arranged to eradicate indebtedness, it would not only end exploitation, but also increase productivity and the general standard of living. Already the co-operative form of organisation had been tried successfully in many countries including Britain, Germany, Denmark and India, and agitation for reform, particularly in the matter of provision of reasonable credit facilities to farmers, began to mount.

Foremost among the agitators for reform was a Dr. Ferguson of *The Ceylon Observer*. He published a periodical called *The Tropical Agriculturist* along with its regular supplement *The Agricultural Magazine*. In the issue of September 1901, the Magazine in its Editorial appealed for the establishment of Agricultural Banks in Ceylon, on the lines of similar institutions established in Germany during the 'Hungry Forties'. In the December issue of the same year there appeared

---

8.   Emerson-Tennent, J., Sessional Paper—Papers Relating to the Grain Tax, Government of Ceylon, 1878.

9.   Ibid.

an article on 'Raiffeisen Banks'. It was obvious that Dr. Ferguson had been per-suaded by the arguments put forward by Sir Frederick Nicholson, who had undertaken a special study of rural credit institutions in Europe in 1895 at the request of the Madras Government, and whose *Report on Land and Agricultural Banks* had made a strong case for the introduction of credit societies or banks of Unlimited Liability in India, similar to the agricultural banks established by F.W. Raiffeisen in Germany in 1846.

There was famine in Germany following the failure of the harvest in the excep-tionally severe winter of 1846-47. Frederick W. Raiffeisen, the country mayor of Westerwald, took the initiative to establish a 'Bread Society' to help the very poor. Realising that there was a permanent state of poverty because of the poor people's inability to obtain credit, Raiffeisen took the next step of purchasing basic agricultural necessities such as seed and manure through the society to be given on credit to the poor farmers. His final and crucial move was to establish a self-help or co-operative society in the neighbouring village of Flammersfeld in 1849. It started by making credit available to poor farmers to buy cattle, but was soon transformed into a credit society or agricultural bank to provide loans for all essential needs. Raiffeisen is remembered for incorporating the principle of Unlimited Liability in the dispensation of credit.

The principle of Unlimited Liability was born out of the practical wisdom of Raiffeisen. It meant that those who joined the co-operative society committed themselves to back the risks taken by the society with their entire assets. In other words, members were jointly and severally liable without limit or restrictions for any debts incurred by the society, to the full extent of their assets, movable and immovable. In the first place, by accepting unlimited liability, those members who were comparatively affluent were prepared to take a rather greater risk, the principle being that this was necessary for the benefit of the less affluent mem-bers, who were in greater need of credit. In the second place, although most of those who joined the society needed credit, the majority did not have suitable assets to surrender as security. The only security they could pledge was their integrity and industry. Thus what in fact unlimited liability did was to capitalise on the sterling qualities of the membership, and at the same time pool the mate-rial resources of all the members, the underlying principle being a sense of altru-ism, mutual trust, and obligation on the part of each and every member. By revolutionising the whole concept of creditworthiness and providing for a unique marriage of social insurance and economic power, the principle of Unlimited Lia-bility not only spells out Social Justice, but consolidates it.

The most vociferous call for the introduction of co-operative societies in Ceylon, based on the German model, came from the Government Agent of Uva Province, J.O.K. Murty. Having worked previously in India and being aware of the success of the Raiffeisen model of co-operatives that were introduced there in 1904, Murty sent a special memorandum to the Colonial Secretary in 1908 urging the establishment of co-operative credit societies for the native agriculturists of the Province of Uva on the lines of the Bengal societies. He also forwarded a copy of the by-laws of the Bengal societies with suggested modifications to suit local conditions. However, governmental action awaited the arrival of Sir Henry MacCallum as Governor, who appointed a Committee of Investigation, called the Agricultural Banks Committee, in 1909, and submitted to it a personal Memorandum recommending the establishment of the type of co-operative credit societies advocated for India by Sir Frederick Nicholson.

Following the recommendations of the Committee, the Ceylon Co-operative Credit Societies Ordinance No.7 was passed in the Legislative Council on 5 May 1911.

It has to be noted that although the German 'Raiffeisen' model was introduced to Ceylon, it was bound to be a blend of co-operative ideas and principles that had evolved in other countries too since mid nineteenth century, especially in England since the 'Rochdale Pioneers' broke new ground with enlightened leadership. As the administrators of the proposed reforms were also quintessentially British with a touch of reformist ideas, there was no escaping the fact that the Co-operative Movement that was introduced in Ceylon had a British tinge, as well as patronage.

Whereas the Rochdale initiative was a reaction of ordinary people who were left to pick up the pieces of the Industrial Revolution, the Raiffeisen initiative in Germany was a spontaneous reaction to a natural disaster in the form of a famine, which affected the lives of small farmers and artisans. However, both initiatives, having been taken roughly at the same time, developed into self-help movements over time, with some common characteristics. It was, therefore, possible to give a definition to a co-operative organisation, with some clearly tested and defined principles attached to it in order to distinguish it from other types of business or socio-economic institutions.

The development of the co-operative movement in other countries also helped researchers and officials interested in the progress of the movement to agree on some minimum conditions that determine the success of co-operative organisations. Briefly, those minimum conditions were identified as: (a) a common, genuine, and felt need; (b) a sense of socio-cultural cohesion within the group; (c) a minimum standard of education, defined in educational parlance as Functional Literacy; (d) availability of persons with all-round knowledge and recognised qualities of leadership; (e) a favourable social, economic and political climate for democratic reforms through legislation; and (f) motivation prompted by a sense of mutual obligation and altruism.

When the Agricultural Banks Committee was appointed by the Governor of Ceylon in 1909, the Indian co-operative credit societies had made some headway, especially in Bengal, which too had to grapple with the severe consequences of a famine as in Germany. Thus the British administrators, responsible for the implementation of the Ceylon Co-operative Credit Societies Ordinance of 1911, were already acquainted with the policies and practices of their counterparts in India. According to Hans-H Munkner, the policy of the Government was one of assistance, concentration on education, advice and audit, and no interference.[10]

H. Calvert who had a distinguished career in India as Registrar of the Punjab during the formative and difficult period of the Co-operative Credit Movement, and later served in Ceylon as Registrar, defined a co-operative society as "a form of organisation, wherein persons voluntarily associate together as human beings, on a basis of equality, for the promotion of the economic interests of themselves, and not anybody else."[11] This model of a co-operative society, described as the "classical British-Indian Pattern of Co-operation"[12], which was later introduced to Ceylon, had always depended for its success on at least the more important conditions being met.

The Royal Commission on the Co-operative Movement in Ceylon obviously had the same thing in mind when it observed: "Co-operation is a delicate flower that does not thrive except in the right soil."[13] The Commission also had no qualms

---

10. Munkner, Hans-H., *Co-operative Law as an Instrument of State-sponsorship of Co-operative Societies*, ILO, Co-operative Information, No. 1/73, pp 8 et seq.
11. Calvert, H., *The Law and Principles of Co-operation*, 5th edition, Calcutta, 1959, p 18.
12. Surridge, B.J. and Digby, M., *A Manual of Co-operative Law and Practice*, 3rd edition, Cambridge, 1967, p v.
13. *Report of the Royal Commission on the Co-operative Movement in Ceylon*, Sessional Paper No 11, 1970, p 325.

in observing: "From the beginning the people in Jaffna took to Co-operation more readily and more enthusiastically than the rest of the Island, and the Societies in Jaffna maintained a generally high level of excellence, although in other districts also there were examples of good societies."[14]

Research has shown the importance of not merely some minimum conditions, but also the interaction of some of the more essential ones like, for example, education, quality of life and leadership.

"It is certainly not accidental that the countries in which co-operation dominates rural economy are those in which rural life is most attractive and the level of culture and social responsibility is highest. How far this is the direct result of co-operation it would be more difficult to demonstrate. It would perhaps be truer to say that the impulse towards co-operation in the economic field tends to go with active professional interests, social and civil responsibility, and cultural appreciation. At least it has been shown that leadership in any of these fields almost invariably goes with leadership in others."[15]

The essential ingredients for successful co-operative initiatives naturally continued to be dominant in Jaffna even after the Co-operative Societies Ordinance of 1911 was amended in 1921 to allow for the establishment of non-credit societies and secondary supervising organisations. The Royal Commission on the Co-operative Movement in Ceylon emphasised this when they referred to the Moolai Co-operative Hospital Society in Jaffna, registered in 1936, as "a remarkable example of the combination of co-operative enterprise, philanthropy, and public spirit, and a unique society in a class by itself, which has inspired the establishment of similar institutions in other parts of the country."[16]

---

14. Ibid., p 15.
15. The Challenge to Traditional Co-operation, Editorial, *Year Book of Agricultural Co-operation*, Plunkett Foundation for Co-operative Studies, Oxford, 1962, pp 1 et seq.
16. *Report of the Royal Commission on the Co-operative Movement in Ceylon*, op. cit., p 132.

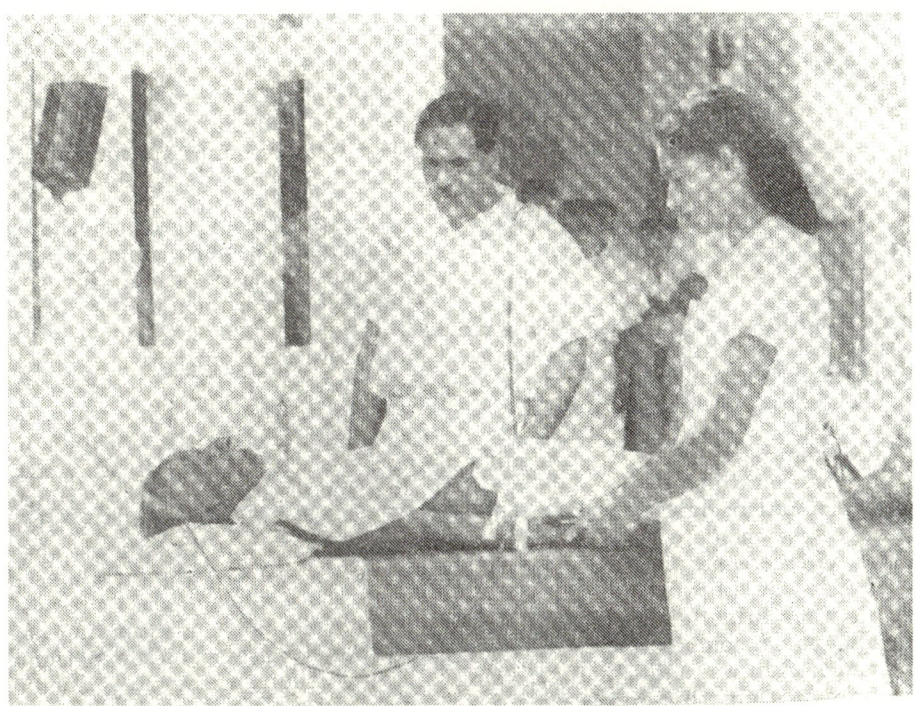

A doctor checks on the progress of a patient
at the Moolai Co-operative Hospital, Jaffna, c.1948.

In the history of the Co-operative Credit Societies in Ceylon, and indeed the entire movement, the period of W.K.H. Campbell's stewardship (1926-1934) was crucial. It was a period of consolidation and expansion of credit societies and experimentation with other types of co-operatives. Campbell pursued a policy of de-officialising the movement. As such he promoted and encouraged the establishment of secondary level societies to undertake supervisory functions of primary societies and special types of co-operative societies to cater to the special needs of the public in general and members of co-operative societies in particular. He also initiated a radically new system of appointing as Honorary Supervisors of Co-operative Societies, distinguished persons who had proved their mettle at grass-roots level.

Higher financing institutions like Co-operative Central Banks emerged during this period, the first and the most outstanding of them being the Jaffna Co-operative Central Bank established in 1929. The message given by Campbell himself on the occasion of the Silver Jubilee celebration of the bank in 1954 explains the background:

"Though Gate Mudaliyar V. Ponnampalam, your President, has been kind enough to refer to my 'responsibility for the organisation of the Bank' I feel that, that is an over-statement of my contribution. Although with the very able assistance of Mr. J.A. Maybin (later Sir John Maybin, KCMG, whose death as Governor of Northern Rhodesia was such a tragic loss to the cause of Co-operation and to colonial administration generally) I did what I could to encourage and advise a group of enthusiasts in what was then a form of Co-operation new to Ceylon, nothing which either or both of us could have done would have produced any results without the genuine and enlightened enthusiasm of those with whom we were working. The Jaffna district had already won for itself a distinguished position in the island's movement, and it was fitting that the seal should be set on its achievement by the formation of the first Central Bank.

"Since I left Ceylon in 1934 news of the development of the bank has reached me in a fairly continuous stream in many parts of the world. The effect has been steadily to increase my pride in having been associated with the foundation of so distinguished an institution. I am glad that this happy occasion is to be marked by its entry into occupation of a building so handsome as to be almost worthy of its occupant."[17]

---

17. *Silver Jubilee Souvenir*, The Jaffna Co-operative Provincial Bank Ltd., 1929-1954, pp 7-8.

The Jaffna Co-operative Provincial Bank in its heyday,
with its Crest displayed in front.

As a matter of fact, the President himself observed on the occasion to mark the
Silver Jubilee:

> "This Bank is regarded as the corner stone of economic progress in the
> North. Everywhere soaring profits seem to have been the order of the day,
> but our profits have not soared because we have always adhered to the tradi-
> tional restraint on profit making.
>
> "Our real purpose is to serve the country by contributing to the financial
> needs of the Province in providing credit facilities for both agricultural and
> industrial undertakings. This has been proved by the fact that the present
> turnover has steadily risen to well over sixty one million rupees. The volume
> of deposits amounting to over two million rupees shows the extent of public
> confidence that the Bank has secured."[18]

---

18.   Ibid., *Foreword.*

The Bank's Crest in detail.

Campbell's modest message to the Jaffna Co-operative Bank speaks volumes for the quality of leadership at all levels at that point of co-operative history. Yet his humility and magnanimity cannot take away his great contribution to the cause of Co-operation in Ceylon; and Jaffna in particular. His philosophy of honest dispensation of Social Justice combined with his meticulous planning was behind the success of many pioneer institutions in the country, including Jaffna.

Tobacco was one of the major cash crops in Jaffna on which smallholders depended for their livelihood. The export of tobacco to Travancore (Malayalam) was a lucrative trade for the farmers for a number of years, until the state government of Travancore began to impose punitive tariffs on imports in order to encourage local production. In practice, it meant that the tobacco cultivator in Jaffna had to depend more and more on the village money-lender or trader, who naturally charged prohibitive rates of interest on the advances they paid to the cultivator to mitigate the risks they were taking, and also bought the entire crop at a price far below the market price. In short, there was large-scale exploitation of the cultivators by middlemen in which big sharks from both sides of the strait were involved.

It was after much thought and deliberation, involving local as well as national leaders, and the backing of Campbell and his officials, that the Jaffna-Malayalam Tobacco Co-operative Sales Society was registered on 26 April 1934, with thirteen members, and a promised loan of Rs.350,000 from the Local Loans and Development Fund. Handling a small crop in its first year of operation, the Society, whose membership by then had risen to 219, was able to pay its members a rebate of nearly Rs.4,000 each. The entire operation was simple and quite straightforward. Having already notified the members of the prevailing market price for the different grades of tobacco, the Society would classify the produce and pay the cultivators an average of 60 per cent of the market price as advance. On the completion of all sales transactions the members were paid the balance due to them, the Society having deducted its actual expenses.

As a direct consequence of efficient and honest dispensation of benefits to its members, the Society's membership rose from 219 in 1934 to 2,231 in 1949, that is more than tenfold in fifteen years, the share capital from Rs1,195 to Rs.197, 061, the Reserve Fund from Rs.166.74 to Rs. 662,675.69, and the rebate or advance paid to members from Rs.266,784.25 in 1934 to 1,079,259.50 in 1949. It also meant a manifold increase in the purchase and export by the Society, from 706,375 candy pounds in 1934 to 2,322,006 candy pounds in 1949.

If the Jaffna-Malayalam Tobacco Co-operative Sales Society was the first one of its kind in Ceylon, it was also designed to be an experiment in the vast potential for co-operative development in the country, especially in the area of member participation, education and socio-economic emancipation.

One of the most difficult problems in co-operative development is to find ways and means of influencing individual farmers or producers to make decisions that collectively determine productivity. Establishing the kind of institutional arrangement with an overall and co-ordinated view could be an elusive, arduous and long drawn-out process, but there was tremendous success recorded in Jaffna, thanks to the quality of the membership, and, of course, great leadership.

Until 1930 the administration of co-operative societies was amalgamated with the Department of Agriculture, but in that year Campbell set up a separate Co-operative Department with the Registrar as its head, and appointed Assistant Registrars to be in charge of the administrative divisions of the country. C. Ragunathan was his choice as Assistant Registrar for the Northern and Eastern provinces.

Jaffna was fortunate in benefiting from the services of Ragunathan, a native of the place who had returned to his homeland after a spell of service in the Malayan Railways. With initial training in co-operative work in Poona, India, Ragunathan took on the task with a great deal of devotion and patriotic fervour. In the first place he set about recruiting leaders of quality and integrity who commanded respect in the community. Secondly, he decided to encourage the establishment of secondary organisations to co-ordinate the educational and supervisory work in their respective areas of operation. He also saw the need for a tertiary organisation to be the focal point for all educational and supervisory work, and give a sense of direction to the various types of societies in the two provinces in his charge. In the third place, since subsistence farming was the mainstay of the people, his policy was to pay special attention to the healthy growth of co-operative credit societies. He identified his next priority as soliciting the assistance of persons with some financial standing and experience for the co-operative movement to take off. Having established his priorities, Ragunathan also made it the general policy of the movement to encourage special types of co-operatives wherever they were needed. With the help of others he set about his task with a clear sense of direction.

Underlying the very nature and purpose of co-operative activity is the fact that the individual member is permanently confronted with innovations, not only in the economic and technical fronts, but also in respect of democratic decision-making, social forms of behaviour and communication, etc., which presupposes an optimum informational level on the part of the members, as well as those who provide the leadership.

The long term solution appeared to Ragunathan to be the selection of leaders from among the intelligentsia, both locally and provincially, who would be able to lead as well as look after the interests of members by developing their understanding, self-reliance, and participation, and more importantly, their potential. He stayed in the background, observed, and listened to others, before spotting a potential leader. That was how he obtained the services of the Rev. A. A. Ward, an American missionary, to be the first President of the Co-operative Central Bank established in Jaffna in 1929. Significant, too, was the choice of the second President of the Bank, the Principal of Jaffna College, the Rev. John Bicknell, succeeded by V. Ponnambalam, Malayan Pensioner with a rich background of experience and expertise, who held office for several years, ably assisted by V. Veerasingam as Vice President. Ragunathan seems to have watched very closely the working ethos of the bank before persuading Veerasingam to become the first President of the Northern Division Co-operative Federation (NDCF), the very first tertiary organisation in the country.

It was the NDCF that set the pace in harnessing local talent for the benefit of the Co-operative Movement. According to the Minutes of the first meeting of the Delegates in the Northern Division held at the Regal Theatre Hall on 3 July 1937, there were present, beside Ragunathan in his capacity as Assistant Registrar, Veerasingam, the Principal of Manipay Hindu College, seven senior teachers, two Malayan Pensioners, one landed proprietor, one lawyer, one Post Master and one Honorary Supervisor—a total of fourteen delegates. The Minutes recorded, "The Assistant Registrar explained the object of the meeting and the bylaws for the Federation proposed to be constituted. It was unanimously resolved to constitute the Federation."[19] Evidently, there was the hand of Ragunathan behind the scene, as it were, going by the unanimity with which the proposal to form a Federation was adopted, and the subsequent election of office-bearers, where again all were elected unanimously, including Veerasingam as President. It only goes to show the respect in which the delegates were held within their own communities, and the much wider respect commanded by both Ragunathan and Veerasingam in the community at large.

The NDCF was registered on 20 July 1937.

---

19. Minutes of the Inaugural Meeting of the Northern Division Co-operative Federation Ltd., Jaffna, held on 3rd July 1937, dated 4th August, 1937.

The following letter[20] from Shelton C. Fernando, Registrar, goes to illustrate the high regard in which both the NDCF and its long-serving President were held:

"London
1st August 1951

"To the President, Northern Division Co-operative Federation, Jaffna.

"Dear Mr. Veerasingam,

I much regret my inability to attend in person your Annual Conference on the 7th, a visit to which we all have regarded as a pilgrimage to the Co-operative North from official Colombo. However, fresh from the International Conference at Oxford, which is just over, I join with you in spirit newly inspired by what I have seen and heard there.

Jaffna came very much to my thoughts more than once. When Sir Malcolm Darling, ex-Registrar of the Punjab, reiterated his faith in the humble Thrift and Credit Society as the integral foundation of the Co-operative Movement, and deplored the tendency to multi-purpose mix-up in other countries with what should be purely banking functions, I thought of your old societies. When Prof A.W. Ashby of the Institute of Agricultural Economics, Oxford, said the world would look increasingly towards agricultural co-operatives for the solving of its food problems, and added that Finance would be the key to development in the critical years ahead, again I thought of Jaffna. Finally, when the Conference as a whole stressed the supreme importance of attracting sound unofficial personnel to the Movement if it was to be virile, I thought naturally of your own example and that of the many able 'unofficials' around you.

I would conclude by conveying to you and your Conference what struck me as the most memorable remark made by any delegate at Oxford last week, viz that of Prof. Ashby when he said in praise of the Co-operative Movement, that the best hope for mankind and the truest test of democracy was not the mere setting up of Parliamentary institutions, which themselves could be subverted to totalitarianism, but the ability of the common man unhindered to create and maintain locally his own social, political and economic institutions; of these the co-operative society, whatever its type, was a precious example.

Shelton C. Fernando, Registrar on leave."

---

20.   Original letter from Shelton C. Fernando, retrieved from the NDCF Building, Jaffna, after it was badly damaged by army raids in the nineteen-eighties.

Later events showed that the appointment of Veerasingam to lead the Northern Co-operative Movement was an act of great wisdom, faith and hope that paid off. On the death of Veerasingam, Shelton Fernando had this to say:

"I came to know Mr. Veerasingam first as a Co-operator. It was my first visit to Jaffna to attend the Annual Sessions of the Federation in August 1939. I learnt that this Federation was then two years old, and Mr. Veerasingam was its first President. Since then for 17 years, almost without a break, I attended the sessions and Mr. Veerasingam was always its President. So he has been till death took him away in 1964.

"In due course I found that he was much more besides being a Co-operator. He was also one of the great School Principals of Ceylon, a devoted Hindu, a keen social worker and also sometime Member of Parliament. Of few in Jaffna can we say as we can say of him in the words of Alexander Pope—

'Not one, but all mankind's
epitome.'

"As a Co-operator he was of the first rank. He was imbued with the very theory and philosophy of Co-operation while deeply engaged in the practice. His book on *The Practice and Philosophy of Co-operation* is perhaps the only work of consequence by a Ceylon Co-operator. Co-operation can be said to have burnt within him like a flame as any who heard his Address at the Federation Conferences would testify. Every word he uttered had the tone of sincerity and imperishable faith in the Movement.

"Therefore, when in 1955 the Co-operative Federation of Ceylon was formed, the choice inevitably fell on Mr. Veerasingam to be its first President. It was a great tribute to him personally when some narrow minds appeared to think that the office should be occupied by a Co-operator of the majority community ...

"Thus Mr. Veerasingam was for many decades a great force for good not only in Jaffna but also in South Ceylon, where he was held in great respect, especially during his days as a parliamentarian. His political and social milieu was at all times above questions of community, caste, or creed ..."[21]

If Ragunathan and Veerasingam were exceptional leaders with charisma and vision, so was Shelton Fernando himself, who as head of the Co-operative

---

21.   *Veerasingam Memorial Number*, NDCF., Jaffna, September, 1965, p 21.

Department for almost two decades went out of the way to reach out to the Co-operative Movement in every corner of the country. There had been many co-operative officers of high calibre like Campbell and Calvert, but Shelton Fernando stands out for his vision of a genuine co-operative base to be the foundation of a truly democratic nation committed to national integration and Social Justice. Therefore, when he died in 1971, the present writer felt obliged to recognise his great contribution by writing an *Appreciation*, which was published in many newspapers and journals. It read:

"The voice that hummed an original tune is stilled. The tongue that spoke differently from the rest is silenced. The pen that wrote the truth is dried. One of Ceylon's greatest citizens, Shelton C. Fernando, whose name is synonymous with efficiency, integrity, sincerity, humility, humaneness, and above all, scholarship and patriotism of a rare order, is no more.

"His last words are of such singular strain in the present context of our country's history that there is reason to take heart that men of the calibre of Arunachalam, Ramanathan, Peiris and Jayatilleke, are not mere celebrities of a rich heritage, but are still among us in flesh and blood, and the country that produced giants of such stature should have reasonable hopes of a better tomorrow.

"Shelton Fernando is remembered as one who made a significant contribution to the development of the Co-operative Movement in Ceylon, with which he was officially associated for nearly two decades. At the Oxford Conference of the early 'forties he was highly commended for having successfully introduced 87 different types of single-purpose co-operatives in Ceylon, a feat unparalleled in any other part of the world. It was his link-up scheme at Palugama which eventually flowered into the multi-purpose scheme of the 'fifties. Another of his outstanding achievements was the establishment of the Co-operative Federation of Ceylon in 1955, which was followed eventually by Ceylon's admission as a member of the International Co-operative Alliance. Mention, too, must be made of the fact that he as Registrar cum Commissioner went out of the way to ensure that V. Veerasingam, the veteran Co-operator of Ceylon and President of the Northern Division Co-operative Federation since its inception in 1937, was unanimously elected as the first President of the newly registered Co-operative Federation of Ceylon.

"A progressive and liberal minded official, he always believed in justice and fair play and recognised merit for its own sake. Unlike his colleagues in the civil service, he refrained from sticking to the letter of the law—he was convinced that a people's movement that draws its sustenance from the people cannot but meet people at their own levels and at their very doorsteps. As an enthusiastic innovator, he experimented with the provision of a number of services through co-operative effort, all of them unique. Pawn-broking by rural co-operatives, housing schemes for the middle and lower classes, including the most successful Kiribathgoda Housing Scheme, Thrift Societies, a Theft Prevention Society for cardamom growers, and a Holiday Home for Co-operative Officers are some examples of his ingenious capacity for innovation. He took co-operation even to the long-neglected Veddha settlements of Bibile. Casting a glance on Jaffna, he encouraged the establishment of a Plantain Sales Society and also an Industrial Society for smithy works at Neervely, a Motor Boat and Ferry Service Society for the Islands, a Motor Service Society for the northern parts of the Jaffna Peninsula, a Bread Society at Atchuvely, Agricultural Production and Sales Societies, Dairy Societies, Textile and Fisheries Societies, to mention a few. Also important were Unions of these primary societies that were formed in due course, to deliver better services to their members as well as the public.

"The Home Ministry gained what the Co-operative Department lost when he was appointed Permanent Secretary to the Ministry of Home Affairs in 1956, in which capacity he functioned till he retired in 1961. But his love for the Co-operative Movement continued, and his advice was availed of by many, including the Co-operative Commission of 1968-70.

"As a classical scholar of repute and a prolific writer, he brought to bear a refreshing style in his Administration Reports. All citizens of this country bow in reverence to the memory of Shelton C. Fernando, a noble and great son of the soil."[22]

With substantial provision for education and training, and supervision and rectification, the NDCF had indeed grown to maturity by the time the Royal Commission held its first public sittings in Jaffna at Veerasingam Hall, NDCF Building, on 11 February 1969. Dr. A.F. Laidlaw, Chairman of the Commission, began the session by remarking: "We are very conscious of the fact that we are meeting in what has been for a long time the stronghold of the Movement. You have been pioneers. We hope to profit by your experience, wisdom and success.

---

22. Parts of the Appreciation, considered unpalatable to the Government of the day, were deleted by the 'Censoring Authorities' established in different parts of the country during the *Emergency* of the early 'Seventies.

The proof of the pudding is in the eating, they say. Likewise the existence of good co-operators proves the success of the Movement. Like all co-operators who are human, you must have had your successes and failures, your ups and downs. Your recommendations are clear and concise, though we may not agree with all of them. Your building is by far the finest I have seen in this part of the world. It represents the experience and vision of the Northern Co-operators and shows a great deal of planning on the part of the Co-operative Movement here."[23]

Northern Division Co-operative Federation Building, Jaffna,
incorporating the magnificent Veerasingam Hall.

Unfortunately for Jaffna, it was not to be the end of the story. Already some moves initiated by politicians with vested interests had begun to eat into the very vitals of the Co-operative Movement. The hazards of electioneering and demagogic democracy began to be felt in all aspects of national life, including the Co-operative Movement. The thin end of the wedge of governmental control first became evident with the hasty introduction of the multi-purpose scheme following the consumer drive of the 'fifties. In July 1957 Philip Gunawardene, Minister of Agriculture and Food, issued the following directive:

"The re-organisation of the co-operative structure, I think, is essential not only for the healthy growth of the movement but even for its continued existence. The re-organisation I envisage is the replacement of the varied types of co-operative societies by a single multi-purpose co-operative in each

23.   *The Co-operator*, Jaffna, 15th February, 1969, p 1.

village ... The main function of the village co-operative will be credit, purchasing, and sales. As soon as such a society is established in any village, the
distribution of rationed food-stuffs, the purchase of commodities under the
Guaranteed Price Scheme, and the grant of subsidies by Government for fertilisers etc., will be done only through such a co-operative and only to or
from its members ... In short, the multi-purpose society would embrace all
aspects of the co-operative life of the village except co-operative production
... I also do not propose to disturb the credit societies of unlimited liability
which are functioning satisfactorily. Such societies, where they exist, will
continue to function along with the village multi-purpose society which
would itself be performing credit functions ..."[24]

Apart from putting the small credit societies in an unenviable position, the Minister went on to say:

"I have set the Co-operative Department the target of establishing a multi-
purpose co-operative society in each village within the course of the next
three years. I appeal to the people and to all officers in the departments
within my Ministry and outside it to contribute their share to the attainment
of this target."[25]

It was evident that the Wisconsin-returned revolutionary who had spent his
prime waiting for his hour did not mince words, and that the fears expressed by
Sir Malcolm Darling and Prof. Ashby at the Oxford Conference of 1951, and
echoed by Shelton Fernando in his letter to Veerasingam on 1st August that year,
had at last come to haunt the co-operators.

The Ministerial decree was carried out so punctiliously that by 1958 there were
1,498 multi-purpose co-operative societies in the country, of which only 607
were new societies, but 891 conversions of mostly credit societies. It prompted
the Administration Report of that year to sound a note of unusual alarm—"the
pace seems too fast from cautious co-operative standards!"

There was no doubt that a radical overhaul of the co-operative movement was in
sight, and the independence of the movement was in perilous waters.

---

24. Directive of the Minister of Agriculture and Food, dated 1st July, 1957.
25. Ibid

Writing in 1966, H.S. Wanasinghe, a former head of the Co-operative Department, widely respected for his services to the movement, observed: "The problem
of Rural Credit looms large. Increase of agricultural production lags behind due
to the relative absence of timely input of production credit, production supplies,
and efficient marketing arrangements."[26] He attributed this failure on the part of
the new multi-purpose co-operatives to a number of reasons, the main ones being
the large number of societies that were not economically viable, the predominant
pre-occupation of those societies with consumer activities of an 'agency' nature,
the comparative neglect of Membership Education and leadership training, and
finally and crucially, the increased involvement of the state.[27]

It was merely a question of time before all co-operative societies were converted
into virtual state agencies. The Royal Commission was unequivocal in its criticism of the trend:

> "Reviewing the history of the Co-operative Movement in Ceylon of the past
> sixty years brings into focus one fact above all: Government, acting in the
> earlier period as trustee and guardian, has ended up in the firm control over
> what was intended to be a voluntary movement. This complete reversal of
> roles was brought about partly by forces and trends over which Government
> had little or no control, partly as a result of deliberate moves made by Gov-
> ernment and its officials, and partly by the default of co-operators them-
> selves. Co-operation has now become the handmaid of the State and co-
> operative societies are virtually agencies directed to carry out Government
> policy."[28]

The United National Party in Government that appointed the Commission, following mounting pressure from co-operative interests, was content to pigeonhole
the Report of the Commission (1970), as was customary bureaucratic practice, as
it contained proposals for some form of regional autonomy in the matter of co-
operative development, which would have proved politically embarrassing in
what was an election year. As was feared, 1970 witnessed a change unprecedented
in the country's parliamentary history. The opposition United Front was swept
into office with a massive mandate. The euphoria was reflected in the Throne
Speech of 14 June 1970. It pledged to make democracy a 'living reality' by pro-

---

26. Wanasinghe, H.S., Ceylon—Recent Trends, *Year Book of Agricultural Co-operation*,
     op. cit., 1966, pp 52-61.
27. Ibid.
28. *Report of the Royal Commission on the Co-operative Movement in Ceylon*, op. cit., p.41.

viding for genuine people's participation at all levels. As expected, there were pro-nouncements on the Co-operative Movement too:

> "... the central wholesale trade in all imported essential commodities and in such local commodities as may be deemed necessary will be handled by various state and co-operative organisations ... Retail trade will be carried out through Ceylonese retail traders, co-operative and state shops ... The heavy and capital goods industries and other suitable basic industries will be state-owned. Other industries will be assigned to the co-operatives and to private enterprise ... The Co-operative Movement will play a major role in the economy of the country especially in rural development. My Government will organise the co-operatives into larger and economically more viable units ..."[29]

Apparently, the so-called 'Throne Speech' had been written by some political appointees with Marxist ideology breathed into them, given its quixotic mumbo jumbo.

Proposals for the Re-organisation of the Co-operative Movement soon followed. The question of the independence of the Movement was no longer the issue, with political patronage on the ascendancy.

The Re-organisation Scheme marked the demise of the Co-operative Movement in the whole country, particularly Jaffna where massive strides had been taken already. Under the Co-operative Societies Law No.5 of 1972, organisations like the Multi-purpose Co-operative Societies were converted into large organisations operating in large areas like parliamentary constituencies. Even primary societies like the Textile Weavers' Societies were made to adopt the District as their area of operation. Unions like the Fishermen's Societies Union were similarly forced to operate in largely extended areas, which made them almost redundant.

The Co-operative Credit Societies of the Raiffeisen type, once the backbone of the Movement, had to languish, due to lack of supervision and education, and also as a direct consequence of their functions being overlapped by the much larger and more powerful multi-purpose overlords. As already indicated, many credit societies were taken over, liquidated in the name of rationalisation, or forced to become defunct in a soil not conducive to their development.

---

29. *The Co-operator*, Jaffna, 15th June, 1970, p 1.

The Northern Division Agricultural Producers' Co-operative Union, that had performed yeoman service to the entire Province through its affiliated Agricultural Producers and Sales Societies, by co-ordinating the supply and marketing of local produce, was amalgamated with a primary society at the national level, euphemistically called the Co-operative Marketing Federation.

All the newly created so-called co-operative organisations, beginning with the multi-purpose co-operatives, came to be directly controlled by the government, and in a grand display of mockery, the government also nominated the Presidents of larger organisations like the multi-purpose co-operatives. Jaffna had the distinction of having its Member of Parliament appointed as President of the Jaffna Multi-Purpose Co-operative Society, and the present writer who happened to be critical of governmental meddling in areas such as education and the co-operative movement, largely through newspaper columns and public speeches, was told by the Member of Parliament (President of Jaffna MPCS) in no uncertain terms, that the Minister had made enquiries about him!

Laws governing co-operative societies, including the by-laws, were modified to allow for political interference and to gradually water down the democratic rights of the people and the very purpose and philosophy of the movement. To cap it all, 'Emergency' Regulations were used to merge the Co-operative Banks, including the Jaffna Co-operative Provincial Bank, with the People's Bank that was established in 1961, which by then had been turned into a coveted hunting ground for politicians.

As for the Northern Division Co-operative Federation, 1972 proved to be a decisive year both for it and the institutions it had fostered, when it was forced to become a branch of the National Co-operative Council of Sri Lanka. Its official building with the magnificent Veerasingam Hall, subjected to endless bombardment, stands as a symbol of the shattered hopes and aspirations of the people of Jaffna.

If Jaffna is to recover from its present stage, it calls for nothing short of a rethink of the political landscape of the country, devolution of power being an essential pre-requisite. At the same time, it also behoves its citizens to become effective contributors to economic and social life once again. With the intellectual tradition very much alive, and the rich expertise of expatriates available aplenty, an institution that would greatly help emergent Jaffna, to nerve its arms and serve as a focal point for community education and development, would be, it appears, one akin to the Scandinavian Folk High Schools. With maturity, it should be able to bring about a revolution of ideas aimed at creating an egalitarian society through genuine community participation at all levels.

There is, in addition, a total commitment called for, given the recent history, on the part of everyone involved to put aside old prejudices and grudges, and devote single-mindedly to the task of development. After all, it is population quality and knowledge that matter—the central thrust of Theodore Schultz's Nobel Lecture of 1979—reiterating the fact that education accounts for most of the improvements in the quality of human life, an essential ingredient in development.[30]

Before Jaffna there lies a long and tortuous road of honest toil and genuine sacrifice, but the goal of re-building and reclaiming a proud and precious homeland is worth any price!

---

30.   Schultz, T.W., Nobel Lecture: The Economics of Being Poor, *Journal of Political Economy*, Chicago, 1980, Vol.88, No.4, pp 639-51.

8

THE QUESTION OF SOCIAL JUSTICE

It was seen in the previous chapters that Jaffna had a leading edge in many areas of social and economic life, including education. Reference was also made to some aspects of socio-economic activity where Jaffna was found wanting.

In the Preface to my book *Perspectives in Education* published in 1970, I wrote:

> "If someone were to ask me, 'What is the prime motive force behind this publication?' I would unhesitatingly reply, 'My yearning for Social Justice.' I have no doubt that the quest for Social Justice is the legacy that the latter half of this century would be handing over to the 21st century. The increasing demand for Social Justice must be met if we are to guarantee the working of the new social order. As Karl Mannheim observes, 'The principle of social justice is not only a question of ethics, but also a pre-condition of the functioning of the democratic system itself.'"

I then went on to cite the following lines from Edwin Markham:

> Bowed by the weight of centuries he leans
> Upon his hoe and gazes on the ground,
> The emptiness of ages in his face,
> And on his back the burden of the world.
> Who made him dead to rapture and despair,
> A thing that grieves not and that never hopes,
> Stolid and stunned, a brother to the ox?
> Who loosened and let down this brutal jaw?
> Whose was the hand that slanted back this brow?
> Whose breath blew out the light within this brain?

Is this the thing the Lord God made and gave
To have dominion over sea and land;
To trace the stars and search the heavens for power;
To feel the passion of Eternity?

....

O masters, lords and rulers in all lands,
Is this the handiwork you give to God,
This monstrous thing distorted and soul-quenched?

....

O masters, lords and rulers in all lands,
How will the Future reckon with this Man?
How answer his brute question in that hour
When whirlwinds of rebellion shake the world?
How will it be with kingdoms and with kings—
With those who shaped him to the thing he is—
When this dumb Terror shall rise to judge the world
After the silence of the centuries?

I went on to observe in the Preface, "It is my firm belief that the day of reckoning is not afar, if we brook any further delay in the dispensation of Social Justice."

Regretfully, I am sure the readers will agree, the situation has not got any better with the passage of time. The condition of the masses of people in Jaffna, especially in the villages, is doubly depressing. In Chapter 3, I referred to the excesses of slavery some years ago, which made the British Government to abandon its much acclaimed policy of *laissez faire* and resort to a Proclamation (1821) to abolish the slave-owners' right to maltreat or kill their slaves. In effect slavery was not abolished, but only swept under the carpet to re-emerge from time to time in other ugly forms.

One obvious guise under which it has continued to this day is through enslavement of children of all ages in various forms. While on the one hand it is recognised that the development of the world's human resources is as important as investment in capital goods and services and exploitation of natural resources, the stark reality is that in many countries, including Ceylon, at least a quarter of the children under the age of 14 are not in school. About 50 per cent of those children lucky enough to go to school suffer so much deprivation, and even discrimination, that they are obliged to abandon their studies by the age of 14 or 15.

But what needs to be called into question is the abject slavery to which a vast majority of those children are condemned, either as wage earners for their families in sweatshops and factories, or as domestic servants. But a good many, as the present writer did witness all too often in Ceylon, are taken away from orphanages and other charitable institutions, or from the custody of gullible parents or guardians, to be exploited as veritable slaves in homes, work shops, fields and estates, and even in warfare.

There was no Ram Mohan Roy or Jeremy Bentham, no Gandhi or Subramania *Bharathi* in Ceylon to speak out for the depressed and under-privileged. Unable to bear the plight of widows in India who were forcibly burnt to death on the funeral pyres of their husbands, both Ram Mohan Roy and Jeremy Bentham campaigned tirelessly to end the cruel practice. Similarly, Mahatma Gandhi and *Bharathi* spoke out against the sufferings of workers on the plantations of South Africa, Mauritius and the West Indies, as well as in India and Ceylon. Echoing the sentiments of *Thiru* Valluvar before him, who came from a lower caste himself and campaigned against exploitation of all forms in his ethical maxims, *Bharathi* blurted out in blunt and uncompromising language:

> *Beaten and broken, they stagger*
> *Like beasts in an enclosure,*
> *Tethered to the yoke of labour,*
> *Breathless, in toil and torture.*
>
> *Is there no end to agony?*
> *Is there no cure for trauma?*
> *The bitter tears of misery*
> *Sound the death knell of power!*

In Jaffna, the educated classes who invariably came from the higher strata of the social hierarchy, found it expedient to tolerate, and even condone, exploitation of all kinds at all levels.

How else can one understand the actions of a much-admired Tamil leader—Oxford educated, ex-Professor of Mathematics, ex-Member of Parliament, and hailing from a highly educated and professional family—when in 1968 he attempted to invoke the *Thesavalamai* (The Customary Laws of Jaffna), in defiance of Parliamentary legislation, to prevent the lower castes from worshipping at the historic Maviddapuram Hindu Temple in Jaffna? Although, as it turned out, the Supreme Court ruled against him, it was nonetheless made clear that educated leadership as such played little part in improving the conditions of the under-privileged.

In direct contrast, Victor Hugo wrote in his Preface to *Les Miserables* a hundred years earlier (1862):

> "So long as there shall exist, by reason of law and custom, a social condemnation, which, in the face of civilization, artificially creates hells on earth, and complicates a destiny that is divine, with human fatality; so long as the three problems of the age—the degradation of man by poverty, the ruin of women by starvation, and the dwarfing of childhood by physical and spiritual night—are not solved; so long as, in certain regions, social asphyxia shall be possible; in other words, and from a yet more extended point of view, so long as ignorance and misery remain on earth, books like this cannot be useless."[1]

The writings of Charles Dickens are a legacy to all oppressed peoples of all times. George Bernard Shaw, however, struck the nail head on when he wrote:

> "Had Ibsen, for instance, had any reason to believe that the abuses to which he called attention in his prose plays would have been adequately attended to without his interference, he would no doubt have gladly left them alone. The same exigency drove William Morris in England from his tapestries, his epics, and his masterpieces of printing, to try and bring his fellow citizens to their senses by the summary process of shouting at them in the streets and in Trafalgar Square. John Ruskin's writing began with Modern Painters; Carlyle began with literary studies of German culture and the like; both were driven to become revolutionary pamphleteers. If people are rotting and starving in all directions, and nobody else has the heart or brains to make a disturbance about it, the great writers must."[2]

With the diaspora of recent times there must have been some tilting of the balance of power in Jaffna, and possibly some bursting at the seams here and there. But a society given to exploitation of one sort or another would find it hard to

---

1.   Sinclair, Upton, Ed., *The Cry for Justice*, Lyle Stuart, N.Y., 1963, p 133.
2.   Ibid., p 488.

dispense with it altogether, and might even try to perpetuate it elsewhere in more subtle forms.

I walked alone one sultry day
In tempest and in thought;
I yearned to learn where friendship lay
When something stopped me short.

The foot I trampled with my boot
Was pouring blood on sand,
The stranger soaked in sweat and soot
Gave me his Friendship Hand!

As he embraced me, my surging tears fell to his feet, and mingled with his blood.

The incident took place on the Kandy-Peradeniya Road in the Central Province of Ceylon, when I was a postgraduate student at the University of Ceylon many years ago. I had been to my school in Jaffna during a short break to see my colleagues, only to find that there had been some malicious backbiting during my absence, which had made some of my colleagues conclude that I had betrayed their friendship. No amount of explanation would convince them that it was simply not true.

The hurt inflicted on me, and the damage done to my honour, began to take its toll when one day, completely and utterly lost in thought, and perhaps momentarily in a state of shock and confusion, I walked into the stranger.

It opened a whole new chapter for me. I discovered that the stranger was just another human being who was being exploited by his masters in one of the estates where he was employed as a coolie. I was in clean clothes and wearing a pair of boots to protect my feet, whereas he was soiled and sweating and bare-footed, and hungry. With a laugh he told me that he and his family were exploited to such an extent that the injury I had caused him was a mere fleabite.

In fact, much had been written about the exploitation of Indian immigrant labour, and I had read some of it. It had been claimed by some that about 25 per cent of the migrant Indian labourers died in Ceylon. Writing in *The Ceylon Plantation Gazetteer* of 1859, A.M. Ferguson had maintained that 25 per cent of the 'Coolies', being unaccounted for, were presumably dead. Governor Sir Henry Ward also had written to the British Government that "... many hundreds of these poor creatures perish annually, from want, and disease", and, "hundreds die of actual starvation upon the road." He went on to describe it as "a large sacrifice of life ..."[3]

The unexpected incident that took place in Kandy on that day served to open my eyes to a whole host of problems affecting wage earners everywhere, including Jaffna and Kandy that had had a tradition of slavery. In fact, the backbone of the agitation against the abolition of slavery by legislation had come from the gentry of the Central and Northern Provinces. According to Pridham, slaves were the personal property of their owners in the Kandyan provinces, and as such were liable to perform any services required of them by their owners, however demeaning such services might be, like, for example, digging a privy and supplying water to its user, or carrying a dead body or a palanquin. Pridham thought that at the time of conquest of the Kandyan kingdom by the British in 1815, a substantial proportion of the slaves in Kandy were also insolvent debtors to their owners, most of them having inherited the debts of their forebears.[4]

I soon learnt that my new acquaintance was not an immigrant labourer as such from India, but a descendant of immigrants, with well-established family connections in Jaffna. He was compelled to work on the estate of his overlords because of the debts that had accrued over three or four generations. He said that he was working hard in order to educate his three children, so that they could eventually pay off the debts and seek other avenues of employment. He himself, he said, was trying to acquire some knowledge through education in his limited spare time to free himself from the shackles of deprivation, and pleaded for help and guidance.

That deprivation is a misfortune, and not a sin, or a punishment for past actions, accepted though by the vast majority of the people with a voice in government, it has not yet been realised by the majority who wield power that any attempt to remedy the situation calls for both political will and voluntary and collective action. The crucial role of parent or adult education in a country like Ceylon cannot be overemphasised.

However educated they might be in their own right, about the only thing of which parents can be sure is that the world of their children and grandchildren is vastly different from that of their own. The beliefs and behaviour patterns of one

---

3.   Colonial Office, 54/347, No.131, London, 15th November, 1858.
4.   Pridham, C., *A Historical, Political and Statistical Account of Ceylon and Its Dependencies*, London, 1850, Vol.2, pp 223 ff.

generation become inappropriate and indeed irrelevant in the next. Parents and all adults for that matter need to be educated to adapt to new, unexpected and indeed unknown situations.

Dobbs had already asserted in unmistakable terms, that on the eve of the Industrial Revolution and the years following, it came to be recognised, "first in practice and then in theory, that the problems of progress were problems of education." One of his citations was Marshall's *Rural Economy of Yorkshire* (1788):

> "Marshall's account of the township of Pickering—with its numerous yeomanry who have recently dissolved the partnership of the open-field by mutual agreement, while retaining a consistent control of their common affairs—is the picture of a community which comes within measurable distance of reorganisation on modern co-operative principles. In different parts of the North at this period we seem to find the materials which formed the basis of rural co-operation in Denmark in later years, in a society similarly constituted and among men of the same northern breed. We shall discover, too, the germ of intellectual interests, which might have found expression in something akin to the Danish Folk-Colleges."[5]

The Folk High School of Denmark which in course of time spread to other Scandinavian countries, was born of the conviction of clergyman-poet, Nicolai Frederik Severin Grundtvig (1783-1872), hailed as the greatest psalmist since David. He was without doubt the greatest intellectual force of his time, to whom the 'living word' was much more important than 'dead learning', as he put it, to serve as a 'spiritual fortification' against forces from within and without.

In recent times the Swedish schools have been attracting much attention in view of their relevance to the needs of the community at large, and their greater emphasis on study groups, covering a wide range of subjects, like science and sports, labour and religion, temperance and technology, and a variety of social and economic issues. In other words, it is increasingly being realised that with more and more demands on the individual in contemporary society, education must come up with a positive package of solutions.[6]

---

5.   Dobbs, A.E., *Education and Social Movements* 1700-1850, op. cit., pp 7, 38-39.
6.   Paramothayan, K., *Perspectives in Education*, op. cit., pp 160-65.

Donald Oliver sees the central problem of education as "one of creating balance between the primal and modern aspects of human community, systems of thought, and personality. This means creating balanced participation among primal social forms (family and community) and the modern social form of the corporate organization; creating a balance between an ultimate sense of religio-philosophical meaning and the sceptical sense of choices we associate with 'scientific thinking;' and creating a balance between efforts to maximize the potential development of each individual and recognizing the necessity and value of diversity among humans, even in such sensitive areas as intelligence, motivation, and social responsibility ..." Arguing the case for a 'positive culture', Donald Oliver sees the central challenge as "inventing social institutions in which primal and modern elements of human evolution are allowed expression in non-destructive and non-competitive ways; or in which the modern and primal are integrated within a common setting."[7]

It appears that Jaffna is at the cutting edge of history where important decisions need to be made rather urgently, and indeed collectively. It needs an institution not only to instruct, but also to show how to live; not only to think positively, but also to work for the vast majority on the edge of poverty. Only such an institution can cater to the needs of all the people in all the villages by teaching them the techniques of production and marketing, improvement of their housing and sanitation, and above all, the enhancement of the quality of their life.

But as Bishop David Sheppard has warned, "the call for justice jars on many ears. To those who broadly believed the status quo to be a just one it seems more wounding than the demand for charity or welfare." Citing the evidence of community development workers like T.R.Batten, Bishop Sheppard went on to emphasise the importance of professional and local leadership, respect for people's ability to think and act for themselves, and community programmes that recognised the limitations on their resources, with a clear recognition of institutions that matter for law, order and justice in a society.[8] His message of love and hope is particularly relevant to Jaffna, where the vast majority are said to go to bed hungry, with the government believed to be using international aid of all sorts to purchase more and more deadly weapons to be used against the general

---

7.   Oliver, W.D., *Education and Community—A Radical Critique of Innovative Schooling*, McCutchan Publishing Corporation, N.Y., 1976, pp 124-28.
8.   Sheppard, D., *Bias To The Poor*, Hodder and Stoughton, London, 1983, pp 15, 190 & 197.

population in order to quell any opposition. Caught between the devil and the deep sea, literally too, many Tamils are said to be hazarding the perilous seas to seek refuge in Tamilnadu in South India, or in the case of the better-off, to resort to emigration to other more attractive destinations by all means at their disposal.

The Tamils who gave the English language such enticing words as *catamaran, cheroot, corundum, curry, mango and mulligatawny,* also gave words like *anaconda* for a constrictor-boa, *coolie* for labourer, and *pariah* and *pariah dog* (pye-dog) for the outcast and the down-trodden!

> *The Morning Star whispers to Dawn,*
> *'Tell me that you are only for me',*
> *'Yes' she answers, 'and also*
> *only for that nameless flower.'*
> Rabindranath Tagore

Epilogue

I find the writing of the Epilogue pretty daunting. My initial plan was to draw together the gist of my observations so far, and in doing so to re-examine some of the events purported to have taken place in history. But the history of Ceylon, based as it is on myth and legend built up over many centuries, has been open to so many interpretations and re-interpretations to suit vested interests. The Buddhist clergy have had a long tradition of interpreting history with mythical and mystical ingredients added in different proportions to suit particular palates. Ultra-nationalist elements have never hesitated to exploit the susceptibility of history as interpreted from time to time for sectarian and political purposes. No doubt these forces emerged as substantial lobby groups powerful enough to sway public opinion and wield considerable political clout, especially since independence.

I was on the verge of setting about the task of attempting to separate the kernel of fact from the husk of fiction, when I chanced to listen to the BBC's 'Our Own Correspondent' reporting from Colombo on 20 January 2007. The Correspondent, Chris Morris, started off by describing the idyllic tree-lined Bullers Road in Colombo, which he had always liked ever since he had lived down the road fifteen years ago, when he worked as a regular BBC Reporter. It was on that very road, he said, that the Vice Chancellor of the Eastern University was abducted in broad daylight. The suspicion fell on the main Tamil breakaway group with the knowledge and connivance of rogue elements of the security forces, he thought. Kidnapping of businessmen and others for ransom had become a regular feature of everyday life, he went on to observe.

The most chilling part of the Report, however, was concerning Mr. Mahinda Rajapakse, the President, whom Chris Morris had met fifteen years earlier. Since then the former had gone up the political ladder, ending up as President, but Rajapakse was a different person now, he said, surrounded by a powerful body of henchmen, and desperately trying to establish a political dynasty.

Chris Morris referred in particular to a billboard prominently displayed overlooking the roundabout off Colombo General Hospital, with the portrait of a moustached President captioned 'Our Leader', 'Our President'. What was chilling was not so much the image of the man himself, but the slogan underneath the portrait referring to the Sinhalese warrior-king Dutugemunu of the pre-Christian era, who is claimed to have killed Elara, the Tamil king. The symbolism of the story was potent and relevant, Morris emphasised, for the deification of Dutugemunu was for all intents and purposes intended to send the message that the majority community was determined to dominate the whole country by all-out military victory. Ethnic chauvinism had reared its ugly head in what was a beautiful island which "could and should have the world at its feet!", he regretted.

Jonathan Steele writing from Colombo for *The Guardian* newspaper of 9 February 2007 painted almost a similar scenario unfolding in Sri Lanka. Commenting on the "escalating military campaign by the most hard line government since independence," Jonathan Steele reported that "Rajapakse's picture bedecks hoardings around Sri Lanka in an unprecedented cult of personality. He has taken to visiting Buddhist shrines in a chauvinistic sop to the most dominant of Sri Lanka's four religious communities." He went on to alert the international community to a major tragedy being unleashed in the country, when he candidly observed that almost 4,000 people have died since fighting resumed last year. "Sri Lanka's humanitarian crisis is dire. Kidnappings and disappearances, apparently by the police and allied forces, have resumed in Colombo. The civil war has made more than 200,000 people homeless in the past year, almost as many in the same period as in Darfur, which gets ten times the international attention. Like the Sudanese authorities, the government is using its monopoly of air power to conduct a vicious counter-insurgency in the face of lesser rebel provocations." He went on to say:—

> "The outside world can have a role, and India may be the most important player. Floods of Tamil refugees are forcing it to take a renewed interest in its neighbour. It has warned Rajapakse against trying to split the east from the north, a device to foreclose a viable homeland for Tamils and reject a federal solution that most independent experts see as the only compromise likely to end the war.
>
> "Above all, India is refusing to sell arms that can be used for counter-insurgency. That is the best signal. If he believes he can defeat an enemy as widely supported by Tamils as the Tigers are, Sri Lanka's president is as 'mindless' as any bus bomber."

The Buddhist monks were not going to let any opportunity pass to keep up the pressure on the government to adopt a more hard line stand against Tamils, whom they believe to be foreign invaders; for that has been the kind of history taught in schools and Buddhist *privenas* over several years. It is reported that they have embarked on a non-violent protest, *Satyagraha*, demanding the abrogation of the Oslo-brokered Ceasefire Agreement between the government and the Tamil rebels. Again, most people have been led to believe that a unitary status and sovereignty are synonymous, and that any devolution of governance would be tantamount to undermining the so-called 'sovereignty' of the nation.

The so-called *Satyagraha* campaign resorted to by Buddhist monks, which appears disingenuous from many perspectives, takes me back to the time of my incarceration for having participated in a non-violent protest against the imposition of the Sinhala language, willy-nilly, on the Tamil speaking minorities of the country. One of my chores in the Jaffna Prison, where I served my sentence, was to supply water, twice a day, to an inmate, confined to a 'maximum security' cell. A Sinhalese from the south, he was serving life sentence, so I was informed by the Prison Authorities, for having raided a number of Post Offices at gun-point, and got away with substantial sums of money, gunning down several officials in the process. As a result, he had earned the nickname *Yakkadaya* in the media, which meant 'Incarnation of the Devil', and I was warned to be extremely alert.

Apprehensive to start with, I approached his cell cautiously on the first day with two large containers filled to the brim with water. With his rather prominent bird-like and beady eyes, he beckoned me to get closer, and when I did nervously, he burst out into a laugh of hysterical proportions, which made me get away as quickly as possible. On the second or third day, however, he befriended me with his ingenious smile, and gently inquired why, and for how long, I was being held in jail. When I told him, he burst into a fit of uncontrollable laughter that brought tears to his eyes. By the end of my first week in his company, I felt more confident, conscious no doubt, that thick metal bars separated me from him!

It was in the second week when we felt quite comfortable in each other's company, that he began to speak freely. He explained the many circumstances in his life that had made him commit such ghastly crimes, although by nature he was a kind and caring person—I must admit that I believed him. Very soon we were friends who trusted each other. One day, with a sudden twitch of his face, he admitted that he was going to miss me when eventually I walked out of jail, and I saw his bird-like eyes swell with emotion. It was then that he adopted a serious and rather philosophical stance, looked me straight in the eye and said very bluntly: "I know my people only too well—the Sinhalese are simply incapable of understanding the significance of non-violence, or your *Satyagraha*; the only language that they will understand is force or aggression!" I told him that I did not agree with his sentiments, although I thought they were the result of his own difficult circumstances.

The Sunday Times that published the account of my experiences in prison gave it the rather alluring caption, *Ganja in Prison*, for I had also written about the clandestine dealings in *Ganja*, or marijuana among inmates, involving not a few prison officers; it caused me some embarrassment, as most officers had been very kind to me during my sojourn behind bars!

Nevertheless, I have always treasured the memories of my encounter with *Yakkadaya*. His candid observations were brought home to me only two years later, when the army used brute violence to break up a non-violent demonstration in Jaffna against the 'Sinhala Only' Act, during which many civilians were bludgeoned to death, or maimed for life. A few years later, when I was already out of the country, a peaceful gathering in Veerasingam Hall was rudely disrupted by the army, and hundreds of civilians were killed or seriously injured in the mêlée. Not satisfied with the chaos and carnage inflicted, the army went on a rampage, deliberately destroying some outstanding landmarks in Jaffna, including the NDCF Building with its popular Veerasingam Hall, the Public Library and the adjoining Open Air Theatre, and the Sports Stadium. Gradually, the raids were extended to private houses, businesses, schools and the hospitals; even some places of worship. As was seen in the accounts of the two foreign correspondents quoted at the beginning of the Epilogue, the atrocities continue to this day, made even worse by indiscriminate air attacks and severe disruption to civilian life, including supplies of food and medicines in the areas affected. Surprisingly, as the correspondents rightly observed, it gets comparatively little coverage in the international media. Meanwhile, the Tamils continue to pay a heavy price for the 'Independence' they had so relentlessly pursued ever since the halcyon days of the Youth Congress in the 'twenties!

It is indeed highly ironical that while President Mahinda Rajapakse was addressing the annual sessions of the International Labour Organisation (ILO) in Geneva recently, taking the rare opportunity to eulogise on the vast strides taken in his country since and before independence, to improve the living conditions of its citizens; and, while Sri Lanka's Ambassador to the United Nations was elected as Vice President of the UN Human Rights Council for 2007-08, Sri Lanka was ranked as the 25th 'Worst State' in the World's Failed States Index for 2007, involving 177 countries. Sudan ranked first, Iraq second, Somalia and Zimbabwe third and fourth respectively. According to the rankings based on twelve indicators of instability recognised by a body of independent international observers, some of the countries that performed better than Sri Lanka are the Republic of Congo, Liberia, Lebanon, Malawi, Rwanda, Syria, Cambodia, Angola and Iran! It is feared that Sri Lanka will fare even worse next year given the rapid deterioration witnessed on several fronts.

At the same time, it is reported that over the last decade, more than Rs. 1404 billion was spent on 'Defence', although the country was not at war with any other country. Of this so-called 'Defence Expenditure', the largest amount of Rs. 244 billion was spent last year alone, as against Rs. 175 billion the previous year, and only Rs. 62 billion in 1996. Obviously, this is a blatant slap on the face of International Aid Donors!

Be that as it might, the situation in the country has deteriorated to such an extent that the people in the North and East are especially vulnerable, and many, particularly the destitute and the elderly, are reported to be simply dying of malnutrition and starvation.

In order to get an accurate and up-to-date picture of the situation, I wrote to a reliable source in Jaffna on 12 December 2006. Although my letter was sent by Air Mail as usual, it was received by the addressee only on 5 May 2007, that is, after five months! To apprise me of the situation as requested by me, my source wrote from Colombo on 20 May 2007. I received the letter on 3 July 2007—I simply cannot think of a similar situation in any other country, especially one that does not miss an opportunity to parade its credentials—in particular in such areas as the improvement of working conditions, fundamental human rights and, of course, human dignity.

A clearer picture is now emerging. The main trunk road between Colombo and Jaffna, the A9, was closed by the authorities on 11 August 2006, and remains closed to date. As intended, it had resulted in an acute shortage of essential food items, medicines, and petrol in particular that has virtually paralysed the entire transport network in the Northern Province, causing virtual economic collapse. As a consequence, there has been on average a five-fold increase in the prices of essential food commodities. For instance, the price of a kilo of rice has gone up from Rs. 40 to Rs. 200, of sugar from Rs. 36 to Rs. 180, and an egg that cost Rs. 8 before now costs on average Rs. 50! But other essential food items such as baby milk powder and malted milk are hard to come by, costing, if at all available, as much as Rs. 1000 per item.

The current situation, as can be gauged, is that aid agencies as well as India are sending basic food supplies by ship to the North, although subjected to attacks from the army and the navy, as well as armed militia representing various interests. Where there is a collapse of civil order and security, it is almost impossible to establish the real culprits, particularly when rogue elements are reported to have infiltrated even government forces.

One fact emerges though above everything else—to circumvent the cycle of violence and sheer deprivation, thousands are fleeing the country, but the vast majority, the poor, the destitute and the vulnerable are forced to face an uncertain and hopeless future. With the re-emergence of the Dutugemunu saga after thousands of years of fictional exaggerations, the picture is indeed dismal.

Rabindranath Tagore wrote in his *GITANJALI* (SONG-OFFERINGS):

> "Prisoner, tell me who was it that wrought this unbreakable chain?" "It was I," said the prisoner, "who forged this chain very carefully. I thought my invincible power would hold the world captive leaving me in a freedom undisturbed. Thus night and day I worked at the chain with huge fires and cruel hard strokes. When at last the work was done and the links were complete and unbreakable, I found that it held me in its grip!"

It looks as if the government of Sri Lanka has chosen the path of self-imprisonment. On the one hand, they do not want to cater to the fundamental rights and basic human needs of minority communities in the country, and on the other, they do not wish to devolve power either. It is analogous to those parents who do not wish to take any responsibility for their children's well being, but at the same time resort to erecting artificial barriers for those children to fend for themselves. It is high time the international community open their eyes to the tragic situation that has been unfolding in Sri Lanka ever since independence, and take timely measures to halt the descent to anarchy and eventual genocide of unprecedented proportions. Already there have been experiments with the closure of erstwhile channels of communication and vital routes of food supply, and reports of paternalistic boasts by the President that he is supplying food, medicine and other basic needs to the people in the Tamil areas. Aid agencies have had to step in and find alternative routes by sea to meet the basic needs of communities affected by indiscriminate air attacks. A major tragedy is in the making, and ironically, a lot of foreign aid is pouring into the country on 'humanitarian' grounds! I understand that former U.S. Presidents George Bush and Bill Clinton are as much concerned about it as India, who incidentally declined any foreign aid following the 2004 Asian Tsunami disaster.

To return to the Dutugemunu-Elara episode resurrected from time to time, Ludowyk sees it as "an important part of the story of Ceylon. Basically he is the first king through whom the *gloire* of the Sinhalese nation is expressed." Referring to the *Mahavamsa*, which first narrated the story of the duel between Dutugemunu and Elara, he says that Mahanama, the author of the *Mahavamsa*, "hammered out its ultimate shape. In it will be felt the hopes and fears of the *bikkhus* of the Mahavihara at that moment engaged in 'war' with sectarian *bikkhus*; the wish for a strong king who would at the same time be a champion of orthodoxy and amenable to their control; the remembrance of civil war and invasion only to be withstood by the hero."

Those sections of the *Mahavamsa* which narrate Dutugemunu's heroism "are epic", says Ludowyk:—

> "Having praised the justice of Elara, the Tamil king, and attributed it and his miraculous powers to his abstention from walking in the path of evil in spite of his false beliefs, the chronicle asks the rhetorical question: 'How should not then an understanding man, established in pure belief, renounce here the guilt of walking in the path of evil? The statement that Dutugemunu became king when he had slain Elara is ostentatiously interrupted, and there follows the saga of the Sinhalese king—his ancestry, his birth, childhood, his triumphant war against the *Damilas*, his slaying of Elara, and his devotion to Buddhism ... The story of Dutugemunu is the story of both warrior and the incarnation of a Buddhist novice. The *Sangha* at his birth prophesied for him the kingship of the whole of Lanka and the glorification of Buddhism in Ceylon."[1]

There had been many scholars who had questioned the authenticity of the episodes narrated in the *Mahavamsa*. As I recall, it was a B.C. Law, for instance, who observed in his commentaries on the chronicles of Ceylon, that Mahinda's coming through the air threw suspicion on the account, and this was enhanced by the

---

1.   Ludowyk, E.F.C., *The Story of Ceylon*, op. cit., pp 41, 60-61.

more plausible story that Mahinda's missionary work had been directed to the country situated in the extreme south of the Deccan, bordering the South Indian Tamil kingdoms. He also pointed out that no inscription had been found to confirm the truth of the battle fought by Dutugemunu with Elara. Nor did the *Dipavamsa* that preceded the *Mahavamsa*, and provided the latter with much of the legendary material, refer to a war between Elara and Dutugemunu, who has emerged as the national hero of the Sinhalese.

The Sinhalese people, influenced largely by the Pali chronicles and their commentators from time to time, have shown an insatiable appetite to establish connections with dynasties of the northern regions of India, in order to claim an Aryan ancestry, and by implication, racial superiority. The situation was exacerbated by the growth of ultra-nationalism since independence, and the emergence of a class of politicians and so-called historians, who did not hesitate to exploit ethnic sentiments. The views of other researchers and commentators were ignored altogether. For instance, J.D.M. Derrett of the School of Oriental and African Studies, University of London, writing in the *University of Ceylon Review,* categorically concluded:—

> "We cannot altogether neglect certain well known historical facts, although our eventual conclusion must be laid at the feet of historians for their consideration. It is generally believed that Vijaya brought the first Sinhalese to Ceylon about the time of the Buddha, and the Sinhalese language, despite its far from negligible Dravidian element, has been identified as an Indo-Aryan language ... The upper limit for the invasion is quite unknown except to legend; and the language has developed in isolation, and only a small fraction of the present Sinhalese may be even in part descended from Indo-Aryan speakers ...
>
> "It seems that the Sinhalese were a people of pre-dominantly non-Aryan descent, with a way of life substantially identifiable as akin to that common in modern South India ... Of course, the Sinhalese were not Aryans. From whence, then comes the notion that their descendants are? This presents no difficulty. The Buddhists referred to any respectable member of the *Sangha* as an *Arya* and that usage must have been common among the former Buddhist world. Moreover the Dravidians were used to refer to the non-Dravidians as Aryans."[2]

---

2.   Derrett, J.D.M., *University of Ceylon Review,* Vol. Xiv, 3&4, 1956, pp 147-49.

It is indeed irresponsible, and even mischievous, for basic textbooks used in schools, in subjects such as history, geography and civics, to have resorted to perpetuating the notion that the Sinhalese were a different and superior race, and that the Tamils in particular were invading foreigners. Witness, for instance, some of the information fed to foreign tourists by a leading hotel in contemporary Colombo:—

"Sri Lanka's geographic position and its natural resources have its roots in our heritage. The rhythm of a primitive drumbeat, the sparkle of a sapphire and the spice of savoury curry are all a part of this isle of paradise.... Sri Lanka could be best summed up by its shape and substance when called the 'Pearl of the Indian Ocean.'

"The Sri Lankan population consists of four major groups:

Sinhalese—The arrival of Prince Vijaya and those who followed him created the nucleus of today's Sinhalese inhabitants. The Sinhalese form 74% of the population and are mainly Buddhists.

Tamils—Tamils originated from the Indian sub-continent. Tamil migration largely occurred in the 19th century when the British needed labour to work on the tea plantations, because the Sinhalese regarded themselves as farmers. They form 18% of the population and are mainly Hindus.

Muslims—In the 11th century trade in the Indian Ocean attracted many Arabs. The Muslims have maintained their identity mainly through religion and their customs. They form 7% of the population.

Burghers—When the Portuguese and Dutch colonisation ended not all of them left our shores. These descendants are collectively known as the Burghers ... In 1956 a large majority of the Dutch Burghers left for Australia. Burghers now form 2% of the population and are mainly Christians."

Readers can no doubt discern the subtle nature of propaganda resorted to, in the name of ultra-nationalism, through thought control of successive generations. Students of Comparative Education would know that since the inauguration of the state system of education in Germany in 1806, there was a gradual and virtual control of textbooks, curricula and training of teachers. A decree of 1844 made inspection of books used by teachers in training mandatory. This gradually paved the way for thought control, and political indoctrination. In 1889 the German government laid it down unequivocally that German history must be taught with such precision, as to show that the power of the state alone could protect the individual; how Prussia's kings had exerted themselves to raise the conditions of the workers, and how considerably and constantly in the country, the wages and conditions of the working classes had improved under monarchic protection. The Nazis did not wait long to complete the edifice. They brought education under the control of the Reich Minister, who made the National Teachers' League introduce Nazi propaganda into the curriculum. If subjects like history were perverted, it is understandable, for they easily lend themselves to indoctrination. But in Germany even arithmetic books included, for instance, a table giving the sum of money paid annually by the State for elementary and secondary school children, and for lunatics. Then the child was told that there were 200,000 lunatics in Germany, and asked to calculate how much they would cost the State each year, and that a lunatic was an expensive liability. Other problems to be worked out dealt with the Jews and the Gypsies.

In a similar pursuit, the Government of Ceylon assumed full responsibility for the control of all the school textbooks within ten to fifteen years of independence. It shocked the nation, especially the minority communities, which prompted Professor J.E. Jayasuriya, Head of the Faculty of Education at the University of Ceylon, to sound a note of warning:

> "Belief in his own genius has made the bureaucrat prescribe in very minute detail, by means of so-called course guides, what every teacher should say and do in the classroom, the questions he should ask and the answers that he should receive. Absolute conformity is insisted upon and no deviation is permitted. Moreover, it is proudly claimed that to repeat the same words in every classroom is the surest means of ensuring equality of educational opportunity in all the schools in the island ...
>
> "Thought control of the pupils is attempted also through the government textbook monopoly ... Many who had never published any work at all, not even an article in a school magazine, were crowned as authors overnight, and the entire school population of the country had to use the books written by these authors. Rank careerism made the authors try to advance political ideologies and personalities through the books ... The deficiencies in the government textbooks are so many that an entire book would be needed to list them."[3]

---

3.   Paramothayan, K., *Perspectives in Education*, op. cit., pp 174-75.

I happened to sit the Ceylon Senior School Certificate Examination barely two months before independence, and *The Jungle Tide* by John Still was one of the textbooks prescribed for English Literature, one of my favourite subjects. I can still easily recall some of his interesting observations about the Holy Mountain and the valley where the elephants go to share their secrets and die. However, I managed to obtain a copy of the book in order to revisit some of the pictures I had visualised as a young boy. That there was a pre-Sinhalese cum Tamil culture that thrived in Ceylon since pre-historic times was made abundantly clear to me. It is also amenable to logical reasoning, given that a mere 22 to 25 miles separate the island of Ceylon from the Indian mainland; and that people from not only India, but other neighbouring countries as well, would have migrated to the island in large numbers for historical, political, geographical, geological or economic reasons.

John Still, who was later described by Harry Williams as "one of the most expert foresters among Europeans that Ceylon has known" (Vide *CEYLON, Pearl of the East*, op.cit., p.181), puts the picture in perspective when he writes in his own inimitable style:

> "When one reflects how India has been invaded over and over again from lands to the northward, and when one considers the shape of India, tapering to a point as though formed for a funnel to fill Ceylon, and how races lose their vigour in the tropics and are driven forward by more vigorous northerners, it is difficult to resist the conclusion that Ceylon's water-holes hold the history of many invasions. The Straits are narrow and easily crossed, and there is no case of going on, for the next land to the south is the Antarctic."[4]

Very often John Still refers to the jungle people, the Veddhas, and "submerged traces of pre-Buddhist culture of many kinds that should be collected before it is too late." Observing that even the best Sinhalese trackers have a word of respect for the Veddha, whose high caste they admit, and whose race they consider to be older than their own, he also speaks about the many stones he had discovered with cobras (*Nagas* in Tamil) neatly carved on them; and frequent references in early Sinhalese literature to a people called the Nagas who had lent their name to the northern parts of Ceylon at least as early as the time of Ptolemy (c.90-168 A.D.), for he gave them a place on his map. "This is one of the frequent glimpses

---

4.   Still, J., *The Jungle Tide*, William Blackwood and Sons, London, 1930, p 202.

we get in the jungle," he says, "of tribes that were old when the Sinhalese were new."[5]

Referring to the ancient Veddha people, Harry Williams added in his book cited above, that "many of them have intermarried, near villages and along the coast, and are only faintly distinguishable from the ordinary Sinhalese and Tamil village communities into which they have been received. These have abandoned part of their jungle ways, and although keeping their Veddha ancestry proudly to the forefront, live the life of ordinary villagers. Then, too, there is a belief ... that a large section of the original race—Yakkas, Rakshas, Nagas—were men of culture and wealth who were absorbed into the Sinhalese nobility. One theory goes so far as to claim that the Kandyans, the men of the mountains, are all descendants of Veddha aristocracy. Certainly all Sinhalese, whatever their rank, are proud of Veddha blood ..." He goes on: "Their history is of a negative but persistent kind which provokes speculation, for they have inhabited Ceylon for millenniums, and although there is some reason to believe that they are related to the Gonds of southern India, there is no certain evidence of this, nor of their arrival in Ceylon. Spittel suggests (R.L. Spittel in *Wild Ceylon*) that they lived in Lanka before it was split off from India at all. Certainly no records or even legends exist which speak of the island without them." (Ibid. p.172.)

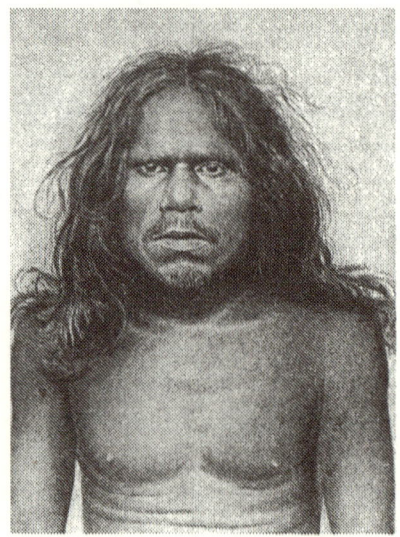

---

5.   Ibid., pp 89-90, 97.

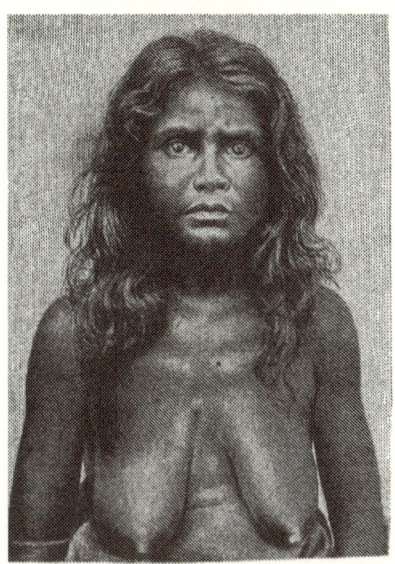

Two very early photographs of a Veddha man and woman, courtesy of
F. and P. Sarasin, which first appeared in 1886. They were later repro-
duced in *Ethnology*, by Dr Michael Haberlandt, 1900, published at 29 &
30 Bedford Street, London.

In *The Jungle Tide* John Still also writes about the three districts of the Northern
Province; he speaks of the many inscriptions found in the *Wanni*, the Dry Zone
area largely representing the present-day Vavuniya District, which are nearly
always simple records of grants of land or other gifts donated to the Buddhist
Order, with the names of the donors invariably inscribed on them. He observes
that they are "still clear to read two thousand years after their chisellers have
gone."[6] How sharp his observations were has been borne out by subsequent
research. Tamil words are encountered in many of these inscriptions. For
instance, the word *Parumaka, Perumakan* in Tamil, is found in many inscriptions. This has been a common word in Tamil, meaning a nobleman or chief. An
inscription in cave No.7 at Vessagiri and another on the Maha-Ratmale Rock
refer to *Marumakan*, which is a common term of kinship in Tamil, meaning
nephew or son-in-law. Inscriptions found in the Avukana and Alutgal *Viharas*
and at Illukavava, Ganekanda and Galwewa, to mention a few, refer to *Vavi*,
again a simple term in Tamil for a tank or a lake. The Tamil word *Kani* for land
is found in the Vessagiri Rock inscription No.1. Some Tamil names in vogue to

---

6.   Ibid., p 134.

this day are also found in many an inscription. Velu in the Netukanda inscription, Yatahalena Rock Temple inscriptions, and the Bandagala *Vihara* inscription, Gopal in the Galgiriyavakana inscription, and Narayan in the Galkandegama inscription are some examples. The Thirupparakunram inscription in South India, which is also a cave inscription, confirms the fact that the Tamils in early Ceylon took an active part in the propagation of the Buddhist religion. The conversion to the Buddhist faith by some sections of the Tamil community perhaps accounts for the presence of Buddhist temples and the discovery of some Buddhist artefacts in the Northern and Eastern Provinces.

John Still also writes about an old city and a seaport that lie buried amid sand dunes off the coast of Mannar, where when it rained, the dunes could be searched for coins and other artefacts from many lands. It was not altogether unexpected, he explains, because at one time this was the chief port of traffic with India, and it was here that many foreign armies landed to raid Ceylon.

Turning his eyes on Jaffna, he writes that he gained some idea of what that ancient harbour in Mannar would have looked like, when he visited the island of Kayts in the Jaffna Peninsula,

> "for in the roadstead there, more than thirty sailing ships were lying. They were of Eastern rig, of Eastern build, and manned and owned by Eastern men; not a single European sailed in any one of them in any capacity. Some had three masts, and some only two, but all were sea-going ships, and between them they visited the coasts of far Arabia and the Persian Gulf, as well as the ports of India and Ceylon. Some, they told me, traded with the remote coral islands in the middle of the Indian Ocean. On the shore two stout ships were being built, and I went aboard one, and was shown round by the designer and head carpenter, a Tamil who knew no English; and as we talked to that well-informed and practical man, it seemed to me that here was a short cut in archaeology, and a more direct route to the understanding of the old port buried among the sand dunes than could be found scouring the sand for coins."[7]

---

7.   Ibid., pp 114-16.

Alluding to the many myths woven around the history of Ceylon, John Still definitely had the last laugh, when he wrote:—

> "Have the Veddhas some ancient memory of a Charles Darwin, and the Somalis of a prehistoric Ronald Ross? Must Wilbur and Orville Wright yield up their laurels to Ravana, King of Lanka in mythical times when the island was inhabited by demons; for Valmiki the poet, singing some think a thousand years before Christ, describes him as flying from the mountains of South India to the mountains of Lanka in a 'bird machine.' Many have been reputed to fly, but this was a machine, perhaps the same fiery chariot that Elijah used, for these stories travel far, and in the woods of Ceylon many Greek myths may still be found: The very landing of the Sinhalese doubles the story of Ulysses and Circe."[8]

---

8.   Ibid., pp 126-27.

A water colour drawing from Bengal, 19th Century, showing
Sita being abducted by Ravana, the demon King of Ceylon, in a
'bird machine'. (Ravana transformed himself into a man with ten
heads and twenty hands to carry out this audacious mission!)

Many eminent Sinhalese scholars see a close connection between the Sinhalese and the Malays. For example, Professor S. Paranavitane writing in the *Journal of the Royal Asiatic Society*, Ceylon Branch in 1960 observed:—

> "Ceylon is situated at the south-western corner of the Bay of Bengal which, on its eastern side, washes the shores of the Malay Peninsula and the northern half of the Island of Sumatra—lands which are the home of the people of Malay race. Should one sail directly eastwards from the eastern coasts of Ceylon, the first land that one would meet after passing the Andamans is the Malay Peninsula; similarly, a mariner sailing westward from a port in the Malay Peninsula or the western coast of northern Sumatra would touch land on the eastern or southern coast of Ceylon. It may, therefore, be inferred that the people of Ceylon and those of the Malay lands would have come in contact with each other in ancient days if they took to seafaring. It was only in certain periods of their history that the Sinhalese people had engaged themselves in seafaring; on the other hand, the Malays have always been intrepid sailors. Geographical considerations would thus lead one to the conclusion that the history of the Sinhalese and that of the Malays would have been influenced by each other ..."[9]

Professor K.W. Goonewardena, writing in Part 2 of the same Journal, noted that a number of Sinhalese family names suggested a Malay connection. Citing such names as Malalage, Malalasekara and Malalgoda, he pointed out that "the fact that many people bearing such names have remarkably Malayan features may not be altogether accidental."[10] Others like Dr. N.D. Wijesekera have suggested a trace of Mongoloid features in the modern Sinhalese population, and cited some Sinhalese words and place names too that can be traced to their Malay origin, e.g., the Polynesian word for canoe, *ORUU*, which became *ORUWA* in Sinhalese, and *SAMPAN* for an ocean-going boat which became *HAMPAN* in Sinhalese and gave the name *Hambantota* to the southern port of Ceylon. They also speak of other similarities like, for example, masks used in festivals and dances, mode of wearing the sarong common among men, invariably with a belt and often with a jacket, and similarities in the female dress codes as well. Some have also drawn attention to the arch-like tortoise shell comb worn by some males as

---

9.   Paranavitane, S., *Journal of the Royal Asiatic Society*, Ceylon Branch, Vol. Vii, Part 1, 1960, p 186.
10.   Goonewardena, K. W., *Journal of the Royal Asiatic Society*, Ceylon Branch, Vol. Vii, Part 2, p 257.

headgear, especially among the older generation, to denote caste or tribal superiority, suggesting a Polynesian lineage.

Be that as it may, in describing the relationship between India and the island of Ceylon, Walter Fairservis, JR made some acute observations, which are relevant:—

"The peninsula juts into the Indian Ocean in an approximate north-south axis; triangular in shape, the southernmost extension at Cape Comorin reaches to within less than ten degrees of latitude of the equator. Ceylon, just to the east of the Cape, is essentially part of the geological story of the peninsula. Adam's Peak, on the southwest of that island, is the first landfall for ships headed for the Bay of Bengal. It has represented 'India' to thousands of voyagers for centuries even though Ceylon is a cultural entity separate from India. Yet even for Indians the peak has meaning. On the summit of the mountain is a boulder, which is said to conceal a divine footprint. For Hindus the print is that of Siva, for Buddhists it is that of Gautama, for Moslems the story has it that Adam, driven from Paradise, stood penance there. Thus, though the peak is low (7,260 feet) compared with India's mountains generally, it has attained a stature unique to the eye and mind. The allusion of legend and story to such geographical features is a commonplace in the Indian tradition."[11]

John Still, however, writing much earlier, had added the Eastern Christians to the list of worshippers, who believed the summit to bear the footprint of St Thomas, the traditional apostle of India. It may also be noted in this context that the Holy Mountain, known to the Tamils as *Oli Padam,* was named *Oulipada* by Ptolemy in his ancient map of the Second Century AD.

Reference was made in Chapter 3 to the Comprehensive Tamil and English Dictionary compiled by the Rev. Dr. Miron Winslow, which had its humble beginnings in Jaffna under the scholarly eyes of the Rev. Joseph Knight, ably assisted by the Rev. Peter Percival and other native scholars, and which was eventually published by the American Mission Press in Madras in 1862. In his Preface to the Dictionary, Dr. Winslow cited Professor Max Muller, who in his celebrated lectures on the *Science of Language*, divided almost all the languages of the world into three main families—the Aryan, Semitic, and Turanian. The Aryan included the Sanskrit, Greek and Latin; the Semitic was divided into Aramaic, Hebraic,

11.   Fairservis, Jr., W. A., *The Roots of Ancient India*, Macmillan, N.Y., 1971, p 3.

and Arabic; and the Turanian consisted of the Tungusic, Mongolic, Turkic, Finnic and Samoyedic of the North, and the Tamulic, Bhotiya, Taic and Malaic to the South. Dr. Winslow showed how according to Professor Muller's classification, Tamil belongs to the Turanian family. He also alluded to further studies by the Rev. Dr. R. Caldwell who had conclusively shown that all the Dravidian languages belong to the Finnic branch of the Scythian family, and had specified 85 words in the Dravidian as having Scythian affinities, 31 as Semitic, and 106 connected with the West Indo-European family, quite distinct from those in Sanskrit. He also referred to Dr. Caldwell's Dravidian Comparative Grammar, which cited 31 words in Sanskrit derived from Dravidian languages, and 25 borrowed by both from a common source, and pointed out that in Dr. Caldwell's opinion, Sanskrit derived its cerebral consonants from the Dravidian. "What is more singular," Dr. Winslow asserted, was that "the names by which the ivory, apes, and peacocks, conveyed by Solomon's ships of Tarshish were known, are the same with those still used in Tamil; seeming to imply that the traders visited Ceylon or India, and obtained with these novelties their Tamil names, *DANTA, KAPI,* and *TOGAI,* as found in the Hebrew Bible."[12]

It would be difficult, perhaps, for those who are not so familiar with the comprehensive history of Ceylon, especially the situation in which the Tamils find themselves, to understand how a people with a rich cultural heritage, who had made Ceylon their home over so many centuries, and contributed in such large measure to the development of the country through many centuries, prior to and after colonial rule, were left high and dry within a few years of independence, with offensive, and often racially abusive labels attached to them. Who will take responsibility for the enactment of such a tragedy on a people who were *de facto* in the forefront of economic as well as educational, cultural and political progress, eventually leading to independence?

Way back in 1965, when I was on the Editorial Board of *The Co-operator*, fortnightly journal of the Northern Division Co-operative Federation, I came across an article in *The Hindu Weekly Review*, Madras, which quoted a statement from Dr. Paul Peiris, the eminent Ceylonese historian, who expressed the view that Ceylon's close proximity to India would have meant that Northern Ceylon would have been a flourishing Tamil settlement, centuries before Vijaya, the legendary founder of the Sinhalese was born. Ceylon's juxtaposition in relation to

---

12. Winslow, M., *A Comprehensive Tamil and English Dictionary of High and Low Tamil,* American Mission Press, Madras, 1862, pp v-ix.

South India is very similar to that of the island of Delft *vis-à-vis* the mainland of Jaffna. A distance of about sixteen miles separates the island from the Jaffna peninsula, in much the same way as a distance of about twenty-two miles separates the northern tip of the peninsula at its narrowest point from the Indian mainland. The inevitable fact must surely be that Tamils occupied not only the Indian sub continent, but also the northern parts of Ceylon, including the adjoining islands, centuries before Vijaya and his accomplices descended upon Ceylon, via the Northern Port of Mannar.

Apart from the *a priori* argument advanced by Dr. Peiris, there are some glaring linguistic facts too that need to be considered. In his Introduction to the Sinhalese Dictionary, Sir Baron Jayatilaka conceded that at least 25% of contemporary words in the Sinhalese language were derivatives of Tamil, and probably the proportion was much larger. It is not surprising at all, since not only in Ceylon, but also beyond her shores, Tamils are the closest neighbours to the Sinhalese!

As a secondary school student in the 'forties when the agitation for independence gained momentum, and as a teacher in the latter half of the 'fifties and 'sixties in different institutions and with different responsibilities, I have had direct experience of getting to know the youth of Jaffna in particular. The lessons I learnt were invaluable tools in my armoury, especially when I was a postgraduate student and a teacher cum administrator in Ceylon, as well as in other countries.

In my experience, the students of Jaffna were the most passive and disciplined in the country as a whole, by any standard; in fact, many observers had commented on it, and even marvelled about it. I can still recall the many occasions when I, like many another teacher, had to rely entirely on the goodwill and co-operation of students in Jaffna, in organising such school events as Prize Giving and Sports Days, Excursions, Educational Tours and School Plays, and later on 'Work Experience' programmes in the school curriculum.

I clearly remember, too, the day when one of my fellow mates in my Hall of Residence at the University in Peradeniya, decided to play Table Tennis. He happened to be fair and rather obese. The cheering that descended into hooting, and eventually escalated to an orgy, was sickening to the core. I decided to go out for a stroll, and as I descended the hill on which my Hall of Residence was situated, along the narrow steps carved out on one of the slopes, I was taken aback when I saw Sir Ivor Jennings, the Vice-Chancellor, ascending the steep flight of steps with the aid of a walking stick. Tall and towering, he confronted me and asked directly, 'What's going on over there?' Lost for words, I stuttered with an inescapable chuckle, 'a chap called Bartholomew, known as 'Bartho', is playing Table Tennis ... and the fellows are cheering.' 'Cheering?' he queried, and resumed ascending the steps in ever-faster strides. In my youthful curiosity, I decided to follow him, keeping my distance, when he stopped abruptly, turned back and said, 'I have never seen this sort of behaviour anywhere else! ... Anyway, which part of the country are you from?' When I replied 'Jaffna', he turned back, looked me in the face, and remarked with a smile emanating from under his short-trimmed moustache, 'Oh! Jaffna is different; they know what discipline means.' I saw him approach the common room, where all the merriment was going on, and I witnessed too the gradual melting away of the 'cheering,' as well as the 'cheerers'. It was not long after, that I happened to read a Bulletin issued by Sir Ivor, and widely distributed, which read:—

> "Driving up and down the Kandy Road my wife and I never cease to marvel at the good behaviour of the boys and girls on their way to and from school. They hurry along the sides of the road in little groups as if they were already grown up; even at the end of the day their clothes are still clean; they never seem to fight or throw mud at each other or roll each other down the banks or fish for tadpoles or put frogs down the necks of little girls. In short, those of us who come from countries where little boys are little devils find Ceylonese children almost unnatural.
>
> "At the other extreme the contrast is equally great. Those of us who spend our lives in universities have never met undergraduates so ill mannered as those of Ceylon; and my own experience covers not only the United Kingdom, but also Canada, Australia, India, Malaya and the U.S.A. I have heard of 'initiation ceremonies' in Canada, but they were on the open campus on one evening and any 'frosh' who chose not to attend stayed away; nor was there such sadism as we had in Colombo. Hooting in Union Society meetings is, so far as I know, peculiar to Ceylon. There is always some obscenity among young men, but until I came to the Ceylon University College I had never heard it in the presence of women. The courtesies which men everywhere (including Ceylon) accord to women are often neglected in the University. The shouting which goes on at University elections is, I believe, unique. The obstruction of corridors and footpaths, and the refusal to move except with discourteous deliberation, even for members of the staff, is the reverse of the practice everywhere."

He regretfully noted that the tradition of the University "is an odd phenomenon, for rowdiness and discourtesy are characteristic neither of the people of this country nor of undergraduates elsewhere."[13]

In early 1971, I was entrusted with the task of training about 100 graduates of the University, when I was the Principal in charge of the Jaffna Co-operative Training School. It was a big challenge and responsibility, but with help of a dedicated and qualified staff, I am glad to say that I was able to meet the challenge. It turned out to be an educational experience for me in particular, for the graduates, men and women, proved to be highly conscious of their duties and responsibilities, and amenable to the code of conduct, discipline and ethos built up in the school over many years of working with, and training, employees and prospective employees of co-operative societies at different levels. I do not remember a single incident of rudeness, rowdiness or unruly behaviour, usually attributed to undergraduates of the University of Ceylon. On the other hand, all the graduate students were co-operative, helpful by making constructive suggestions, and even prepared to participate readily in all the activities of the school, including the provision of special English lessons, 'work experience' slots in the curriculum, and the production of the School Magazine.

In the course of my work, which included some teaching, I was compelled to update my knowledge and adapt new methods, in order to be able to liaise effectively with those men and women who had recently graduated, but were very aware of the almost insurmountable barriers that confronted them in the field of employment. The expression on their young faces showed their fears and anxieties. In that part of the country where most parents devote their entire assets towards the education of their children, the prospect of unemployment would have meant ruin to the hopes and aspirations of entire families and communities, especially when one considers that there has never been provision of any sort for social security, or unemployment benefit.

It was seen in the preceding chapters that missionary enterprise had established a number of good schools in Jaffna. The Hindus too had gradually established equally good schools, and in the competition for jobs, the Jaffna Tamils had a distinct edge over the rest of the country. The relative absence of natural resources like rivers and lakes, and shortage of raw materials, had made white-collar jobs the major source of employment to the educated youth. Moreover, when

---

13.   Paramothayan, K., *Perspectives in Education*, op. cit., pp 93-95.

first the University College and later the University of Ceylon were established, most Tamils were not slow to cash in on the initial advantages that the schools had bestowed on them by catering to the needs of their children, many of whom aspired for prestigious positions in the leading professions. It was also seen that in order to pander to the ultra-nationalist sentiments of the Sinhalese, the Commission on Higher Education had produced a majority report recommending that "in the interests of equality of opportunity," provision for higher education in the University should be made for *at least* six Sinhalese speaking students as against one Tamil speaking student, which was soon followed by the introduction of a quota system based on regional distribution of the country's population. This was in sharp contrast to the developments in India, where the Supreme Court had declared any system of quotas to be a violation of the Indian Constitution, for it saw that the fundamental rights enshrined in the Constitution placed the rights of individuals above those of particular communities, irrespective of their numbers. Paradoxically though, Section 7 of the Ceylon University Ordinance reads:—

"The University shall be open to all persons of either sex and of whatever race, creed or class, and no test of religious belief or professions shall be adopted or imposed in order to entitle any person to be admitted as a teacher or student of the University or to hold any appointment therein, to graduate thereat or to hold, enjoy, or exercise any advantage or privilege thereof."

Even the motto inscribed at the entrance to the University Senate reads, "MORE OPEN THAN USUAL!"

It was made quite evident that once independence became a reality, with a constitution ill suited to the task of nation building, a strident and very aggressive racial ethos began to emerge. Imposing arbitrary quotas was for all intents and purposes an act of gross discrimination, not so much against Jaffna Tamils *per se*, but an act of betrayal perpetrated on the Tamil boys and girls, who had to work much harder than the rest of the students in the country to qualify for university admission, and after graduating at great cost and sacrifice, denied the legitimate fruits of their labour, simply because they belonged to a linguistic group that was numerically weaker than the other. The frustration and bitterness I saw in the faces of those young graduates I worked with way back in 1971 still remain with me, and I have no doubt whatsoever, that those sentiments represented the sheer frustration of a whole generation of students in the Tamil community, faced with a dire situation without parallel in any other part of the world. I saw the nightmare scenario depicted by Edwin Markham in his poem, *The Man With the Hoe*, cited in the last Chapter, assuming even more frightening proportions. Markham's imperishable lines have remained to haunt me over the years, and I wish to share his last few lines with the readers in the hope, that at long last, there will be some light at the end of the tortuous tunnel of Ceylon's long and, often bloody, and distorted history:

> Through this dread shape humanity betrayed,
> Plundered, profaned and disinherited,
> Cries protest to the Judges of the World,
> A protest that is also prophecy!

With the stability of the country under threat, I decided to call it a day, and seek opportunities abroad, especially for the sake of my young children, whose future depended heavily on my very survival and financial security. The threats I received from the government under different guises, and the warnings of some of my fellow compatriots that the police were making inquiries about me in diverse places, such as my old school, St John's College, Jaffna College, and some leading Co-operative institutions, including the Northern Division Co-operative Federation, made me hasten my departure. Even at the airport, the harassment continued, since my luggage, and all items on my person, were subject to a long and thorough search by a senior official, lasting almost one hour. What was more disturbing was, that even personal and private documents, such as letters entrusted to me to be handed over to relatives or friends in the UK, were slit open and read by the Customs official, with an apparently insatiable sadistic appetite. It was much later that I was informed by one of my former colleagues in the Colombo Customs, where I had worked for a short time before going into University, that there had been a pre-planned attempt to detain me on trumped up charges. I wondered then, as I do now, how long it would take for the international community, and international bodies like the United Nations and the Commonwealth, to take up the question of fundamental human rights with the Sri Lankan authorities! In my experience, the governments of Sri Lanka have consistently carried out their covert operations against the minority Tamils at the most opportune moments, when the attention of the international community, including the international organisations, was diverted to major crises situations elsewhere, affecting national and international security.

As B.H. Farmer feared in the Introduction to his book, *Ceylon: A Divided Nation*, the Island Without Problems, which had been held up as a model for all the world, of the way in which a colony might peacefully, and by easy stages, attain full independence, without suffering the communal carnage that eventually severed Pakistan from India, could no longer be regarded as such. Instead of being a model, Ceylon is emerging as a warning to the rest of the world!

The Tamil-speaking people of the country account for a little over 27 per cent of the population. In Finland, the Finnish constitute about 95% of the population, and the Swedes account for a mere 6 or 7 %, but both Finnish and Swedish are official languages. In Switzerland the Germans form about 65%, the French about 18% and the Italians roughly 12%, but all three languages are recognised as official languages. The Tamil speaking population in Singapore represent hardly 10% of the entire population, the Chinese accounting for more than 75% and the Malays about 15%; yet all three, in addition to English, are official languages. It is interesting to note in this context that Singapore was originally part of the Sumatran Sri Vijaya kingdom, which was leased by the British East India Company, on the advice of Sir Stamford Raffles, from the Sultan of Johore in 1819. Although this Buddhist kingdom of Sri Vijaya was discovered by Marco Polo only in the thirteenth century, one cannot fail to see some antecedents to the Vijayan legend and myth woven into the early history of Ceylon, as written in the *Mahavamsa*. Also, place names like Jayapura in the East Indies and Anuradhapura in Ceylon cannot surely be attributed to mere coincidence! Other place names like Madura, Singarajah, Mataram, Sri Inderapura, Martapura, and even Singapore (Singapura), inevitably tend to question the credibility of Ceylon's early history. For instance, the great Scottish adventurer, Alexander Hamilton wrote: "In anno 1703 I called at Johore on my way to China, and the Sultan treated me very kindly, and made me a Present of the Island of *Sincapure*, but I told him it could be of no use to a private Person ..."[14]

It may also be noted that in his letter of 12 December 1818 from *Sandheads* addressed to W. Marsden, Stamford Raffles (Later Sir) wrote: "We are now on our way to the eastward, in the hope of doing something, but I much fear the Dutch have hardly left us an inch of ground ... My attention is principally turned to Johore, and you must not be surprised if my next letter to you is dated from the site of the ancient city of Singapura." (Cited in *Life of Raffles*.)

Belgium perhaps offers a good model for Ceylon to have emulated at the time of her independence. After the Second World War, the main task for the country

---

14. Hamilton, A., *A New Account of the East Indies*, 1744, 2, p 97.

was recognised as one of strengthening the nation by building bridges across its ethnic divisions. The Pact of Egmont negotiated in 1977 recognised three semi-autonomous regions, that of the Flemings in the north, the Walloons in the south, and cosmopolitan Brussels, the capital. Later, however, under a constitution hammered out in 1993, the regions of Flanders, Walloonia, and Brussels were granted greater autonomy, and Flemish, French and German recognised as official languages.

I was fortunate to have had many Sinhalese friends in Jaffna as a student, later at the University and, in fact, throughout my life both in Ceylon and elsewhere. I must admit that they have always been a cultured, caring and friendly people, who have contributed in large measure to the welfare of the nation as a whole. Readers would no doubt also observe, that a significant proportion of the references I have cited in this book, are from some eminent Sinhalese scholars and writers, whom I have always held in high regard. In fact, many eminent Sinhalese, notably P.E. Weeraman, former Director of the ICA Regional Office, New Delhi, and R.H. de Mel, a veteran Co-operator, helped me immensely in my research. My criticism, though, by and large, is directed against all governments and their cohorts since independence, who systematically resorted to a deliberate policy of virtually disinheriting the Tamils, and other minority groups, of their fundamental rights as citizens of the country. As Walter Schwarz of the Minority Rights Group summarised, to which reference was made in Chapter 5, "The Tamil problem is a classic case of a minority emerging at a heavy disadvantage from the relative impartiality of a colonial regime to the hazards of electioneering and demagogic democracy…."

With a substantial proportion of common blood running through the veins and arteries of both Tamils and Sinhalese, one is led to wonder if the administration of the DNA Test, which is commonplace in the contemporary world to solve longstanding claims, mysteries and puzzles, would help to resolve the problem of ethnic chauvinism in Ceylon too. Perhaps, the very few pure Veddhas left could co-operate, by donating their precious samples too, to resolve the ethnic divide for all time!

It is the nation's testing time. The nation as a whole must take responsibility for bringing about the ugly sore in her body politic, and take timely and concrete steps to remove the blemish once and for all. We stand or fall together, and there is no time to lose.

From sylvan *Shanthiniketan*
Sang out savant Tagore,
Embracing all Humanity;
All slaves and slave-owners:
"Bound within narrow domestic
Walls, for Freedom we yearn;
But true Freedom comes only when
The full price we have paid!"

From *Ashram* Mar'thanamadam
The healing peal rang out;
There was *Sevak* Selvaratnam
Echoing lofty thoughts:
"'I have no shoes,' complained a man,"
The golden voice proclaimed;
"That was ... until he met ..." he mused,
"A man without his feet!"

Beyond the veil of Ignorance,
Beyond all thoughts inert,
A world of lovely countenance
Where Wisdom reigns alert,
Where Love and Freedom hold their sway
Appears as in a haze;
All shackles break, there is a way
For you and me to gaze!

About the Author

A long time student of Comparative Education, Dr. K. Paramothayan was well known in the field of educational writing in Sri Lanka, when his book *Perspectives in Education* appeared in 1970, in observance of the *International Education Year*.

Moving to the UK in 1972, he has pursued his passion for Education, while at the same time keeping a close eye on developments in Sri Lanka.

In this book, he sheds unique light on the Jaffna Peninsula in the Northern Province of the country, in an in-depth comparative study.

978-0-595-46733-4
0-595-46733-4

www.ingramcontent.com/pod-product-compliance
Lightning Source LLC
Chambersburg PA
CBHW020432290526
45785CB00002B/817